Media Use Among Postgraduate Agriculture Students

Akshay Khana

Copyright © [2023]

Author: Akshay Khana

Title: Media Use Among Postgraduate Agriculture Students

All rights reserved. No part of this book may be reproduced or transmitted in any form or by any means, electronic or mechanical, including photocopying, recording, or by any information storage and retrieval system, without permission in writing from the author.

This book is a product of

ISBN:

CONTENTS

S. No.	CHAPTERS	Page No.
I	INTRODUCTION	1-21
II	REVIEW OF LITERATURE	22-45
III	RESEARCH METHODOLOGY	46-70
IV	CONCEPTUAL FRAME WORK	71-75
V	RESULTS AND DISCUSSION	76-111
VI	SUMMARY AND CONCLUSION	112-121

LIST OF TABLES

Table No.	Description	Page No.
3.1.1	Information about the district Ayodhya (census 2011).	47-48
3.1.2	Information about the district Kanpur (census 2011).	49-50
3.1.3	Information about the district Meerut (census 2011).	51-52
3.1.4	Information about the district Banda (census 2011).	53-54
3.2.1	Information about University situated in this district.	55-56
3.2.2	Information about selected district and universities.	56
3.2.3	General information of the universities and college with department.	56-57
3.3.1	Variable and their measurements.	57-58
5.1.1	Distribution of respondents according to their age.	77
5.1.2	Distribution of respondents according to their caste.	77
5.1.3	Distribution of respondents according to their marital status.	78
5.1.4	Distribution of respondents according to their family type.	78
5.1.5	Distribution of respondents according to their family size.	79
5.1.6	Distribution of respondents according to their total land holding (ha.) it parent are farmer.	80
5.1.7	Distribution of respondents according to their material possession at home.	80-81
5.1.8	Distribution of respondents according to their communication and media possession.	82
5.1.9	Distribution of respondents according to their farm power.	83
5.1.10	Distribution of respondents according to their agriculture implements.	83-84
5.1.11	Distribution of respondents according to their social participation.	85
5.1.12	Distribution of respondents according to parent occupation.	85-86
5.1.13	Distribution of the respondents according to their annual family income (Rs.).	86
5.1.14	Distribution of the respondents according to their hosing pattern.	87

5.1.15	Distribution of respondents according to their extension contact.	88-89
5.1.16	Distribution of respondents according to general knowledge about mobile mass media pattern.	90-92
5.1.17	Distribution of the respondents according to their scientific orientation.	93
5.2.1	Distribution of the respondents according to their knowledge extent about mass media utilization pattern:	94-96
5.2.2	Distribution of the respondents according to their knowledge extent about educational atmosphere in your university related to mass media utilization pattern:	98
5.2.3	Distribution of the respondents according to their knowledge extent about contact with information sources in your university:	99
5.3.1	Distribution of respondents according to their mass media utilization pattern for the collection of information.	100-102
5.4.1	Correlation coefficient (r) between different variables and Knowledge extent about post graduate students.	105
5.4.2	Correlation coefficient (r) between different variables and Knowledge extent about mass media utilization pattern to post graduate students.	106
5.5.1	Constraints in mass media utilization pattern perceived by the students.	107-108
5.5.2	Suggestion in mass media utilization pattern perceived by the students.	109-110

LIST OF FIGURES

S. No.	Description
1.	Map of Ayodhya district U.P.
2.	Map of Acharya Narendera Deva University of Agriculture & Technology, Kumarganj, (Ayodhya), U.P.
3.	Map of Kanpur district U.P.
4.	Map of Chandra Shekhar Azad University of Agriculture & Technology, Kanpur, U.P.
5.	Map of Meerut district U.P.
6.	Map of Banda District U.P.
7.	Map of Banda University of Agriculture & Technology, Banda U.P.

ABBREVIATIONS USED

A.D.Os.	Assistant Development Officer
B.D.Os	Block Development Officer
V.D.Os	Village Development Officer
et.al.	et all (co authors)
etc.	et cetera
i.e.	That is
Max.	Maximum
Mini.	Minimum
No.	Number
Rs.	Rupees
S. No.	Serial number
S. D	Standard Deviation
ICT	Information Communication Technology
D.T.H.	Direct to Home
F.	Frequency
%	Percentage
MPS	Mean Per Score
T.V	Television
LCD	Liquid Crystal Display
GPA	Grade point average
H.Q	Head Quarter

Chapter I

INTRODUCTION

The word "media" is derived from the word medium, signifying mode or carrier. Media is intended to reach and address a large target group or audience. The word was first used in respect of books and newspapers that is print media but with the advent of technology, media now encompasses television, movies, radio and internet. In today's world, media becomes as essential as our daily needs. Media of today is playing an outstanding role in creating and shaping of public opinion and strengthening of society (Roy, 2015). Media emerged with telegraph and post offices, then the radio, the newspaper, magazines, television and now the internet and the new media including palmtops, cell phones, etc. Now a day, new media is the demand of society which includes online media and mobile media. Online media has changed the face of publishing and advertising over the years, and taken the world by storm. Online media refers to content that is presented electronically (digital media formats) on websites or servers whereby detail is able to be retrieved through web browsers. Thus, it is a form of electronic communication. Industries currently using online media successfully include journalism, news broadcasters, marketing and advertising, commerce, as well as entertainment. (Darryn, 2013)

Mass media refers to any printed or electronic media designed to carry messages to large audiences. Mass media comprises those channels of communications, which are used in receiving heterogeneous audiences simultaneously. Examples of electronic media include radio, television, cinema, interactive multimedia, communication through internet, e-mail, mobile phones among others. Print media include: Newspapers, magazines, billboards, exhibition display, and poster leaflets among others. People use mass media for reasons such as: gathering information for the purposes of acquiring knowledge, personal identification so as to gain insight into oneself, to change the attitudes and behavior of the targeted customers, for integration and social interaction with other people and entertainment (Cantor, 1999). Among urban, unmarried males aged 15-19 in Senegal, 61 % named media as a major source of sexual information, 22 % named school, and 11 %

cited health personnel. Young men surveyed in Bangladesh said they preferred to receive sex education via media sources, with 76 % mentioning radio and 73 % mentioning television as preferred sources of information (Kubaison, 2011). A study on Influence of mass media on adolescents' expression of sexuality and sexual behaviour in Nairobi Province, Kenya by M'imaita, (2011) showed that magazines are the most popular media that provide sexual information (42.6 %). It is further revealed that though magazines are popular, more girls (63.2%) than boys (36.8%) had received sexual information from the television .The breakdown in traditional family systems, urbanization and influence of the mass media are just some of the factors contributing to increased adolescent sexual activity. This high level of sexual activity is associated with risks such as HIV/AIDS, pregnancy, unsafe abortion, economic hardship and school dropout. Studies have shown that adolescents are sexually active by ages 13-19 years. Curiosity, peer influence, expectations of gifts and money and coercion are reasons for early sexual activity among adolescents (Kembo, 2012). In the U.S.A, Several highly publicized murders in schools have alarmed the public and politicians. An average of 20-25 violent acts are shown in children's television programes each hour (Rubin, 1993). Significant association was found between the amount of time spent watching television during adolescence, with its exposure to violence, and the likelihood of subsequent antisocial behavior, such as threatening, aggression, assault or physical fights resulting in injury, and robbery (Huesmann and Taylor, 2006).

The impact of violent media on children and adolescents has been the subject of debate since the advent of mass media, and involved complex interplay of policies, politics, research, commercial interest and public advocacy. The U.S. Congress and federal agencies, prodded by professional organizations and child advocacy group, have for example claimed that violence in the entertainment media negatively affects children and have called for more self-regulation and social responsibility by the media industries (Rubin, 1993). The mainstream mass media (television, radio, magazine, movies, music and the internet) provide increasingly portrayals of sexuality. Studies conducted on the relationship between mass media and sexual behavior suggests that the media keep sexuality on public and personal agendas. Media portrayals reinforce a relatively consistent set of sexual and relationship norms, and the media rarely depicts sexually responsible models. The media are an increasingly accessible way for people to learn about and see sexual behavior. The media may be especially important for young people as they are developing their own sexual beliefs and patterns of behavior and as parents and schools remain reluctant to discuss sexual topics. In the United States, young people spend 6 to 7 hours each day on average with some form of media. Many of those televisions are hooked up to cable and a Video Cassette Recorder (VCR) (Brown& Newcomer, 2010). Two cross-sectional surveys have linked frequent exposure to mass media to sexual intercourse. However, because time order was not clear in these studies, it is plausible to conclude that adolescents who were having sex were also those most interested in sexual content in the media rather than the exposure to sexual media accelerated the adolescents' initiation of sexual activity. The media are full of sexual information and in some of the different kinds of media the portrayals have grown increasingly frequent and explicit (Haggstron- Nordin, 2005).

The importance of mass media 24 May, (2017). the term 'mass media' refers to various forms of communication tools such as television, advertisements, newspapers, magazines and the Internet. These communication tools deliver messages to a large audience. The young people in the research said parental advice is the most frequently sought and useful of sources for making jobs, careers and course decisions than advice obtained from friends and teachers. Formal advice from career talks and services, college open days and prospectuses were judged the least sought after. Young people know very little about the details of work in particular jobs and about the kind of pay and life style that different jobs offer. Boys in particular have very basic perceptions of work that is traditionally done by women. Both boys and girls were aware that male dominated work was better paid than female dominated work, but young people's pay estimates for all kinds or work were very variable and not well related to actual rates of pay. Girls appear to be more open to the use and influence of sources beyond parents including teachers, friends and formal career services consistent with their more social and relationship oriented approach to life generally. The fact boys rely on parental/family sources for their choice of course or career could be due to a more "approval oriented approach" to decision making or simply because they have an anti school tendency. Parents and other family members can be an important source of support for students making career decisions. Family members can be actively involved in assisting with career choices. Personal friends are also possible resources for students and can help provide support and feedbacks. Formal sources such as the internet, leaflets, careers talks, do not feature much in young people's reports of what sources of information or advice have been of most use to them in their occupational decision making of the formal sources of advice, college open days were rated as the most helpful. Overall the relative insignificance of formal career services including and most notably, connections, as a form of contact and source of career advice/guidance. Keeping in view the above facts into consideration this study was undertaken on the following specific objectives; To study the socio-economic profile of respondents. To study the motivational sources of respondents about career preferences.

New Media as a medium of Development Communication: New media or computers entered the Indian Society around 1986. The actual transition in India happened after 1996 when several independent media houses brought out news websites. Today, new media has become an active tool development communication.

E-GOVERNANCE: In simple terms, electronic governance is the delivery of public services and information at the doorstep of the people with the help of computers. E-governance can play the role of a catalyst for sustainable inclusive growth. E-governance uses the Information Communication Technologies (ICT) for planning, implementation, and monitoring of government programs. Through e-governance, government can carry out effective Management Information System (MIS) and get real time information and reports of activities at the Block level. E-Governance has helped to achieve several goals-Automation, Information and Transformation leading to e-Administration-Improving government processes: e-Citizens-Connecting citizens and e-Services: e-Society-Building interactions with and within civil society. E-Choupal: Traditionally, couple is known as the central gathering place in the village, a kind of rural forum, where people discuss, debate and decide on their course of action about some burning issues in the community. The concept of e-Chaupal was conceived by ITC's Agri Business Division, one of India's largest exporters of agricultural commodities. The e-

Choupal model has been specifically designed to tackle the challenges posed by the unique features of Indian agriculture, characterized by fragmented farms, weak infrastructure and the involvement of numerous intermediaries, among others. E-choupals in the digital age share information through the Internet while retaining their pristine, democratic character. The Internet has started revolutionizing the way Indian farmers do business. The system constitutes an Internet enabled kiosk in a village, manned by a villager. He is familiar with computers and known as the choupal sanchalak (one who conducts the forum). The sanchalak acts as the interface between the computer and the farmer. Farmers can use the kiosks to check the current market prices of agricultural commodities, access market data to improve farming practices. Initially apprehensive, farmers have slowly but steadily familiarized themselves with the new system.

New Media's interactivity and easy access have made it a commendable medium for development communication. Launched in June 2000, 'e-Choupal', has already become the largest initiative among all Internet-based interventions in rural India. e-Choupal' services today reach out to over 4 million farmers growing a range of crops-soybean, coffee, wheat, rice, pulses, shrimp-in over 35000 villages through 6100 kiosks across 10 states (Madhya Pradesh, Haryana, Uttarakhand, Uttar Pradesh, Rajasthan, Karnataka, Kerala, Maharashtra, Andhra Pradesh and Tamil Nadu). This enthusiastic response from farmers has encouraged ITC to plan for the extension of the 'e-Choupal' initiative to altogether 15 states across India over the next few years. On the anvil are plans to channelise other services related to micro-credit, health and education through the same 'e-Choupal' infrastructure. The term media is derived from Medium, which means carrier or mode. Media denotes an item specifically designed to reach a large audience or viewers. The term was first used with the advent of newspapers and magazines. However, with the passage of time, the term broadened by the inventions of radio, TV, cinemas and Internet. In the world of today, media has become almost as necessary as food and clothing. It is true that media is playing an outstanding role in strengthening the society. Its duty is to inform, educate and entertain the people. It helps us to know current situation around the world. The media has a strong social and cultural impact upon society. Because of its inherent ability to reach large number of public, it is widely used to convey message to build public opinion and awareness.

The role of media in education is evident today by the number of computer labs, television sets and libraries that have become part of curriculum in most schools today. Media comes in different forms and each form affects the way students learn and interpret information. Media has brought the world closer (globalization) so that now students from different universities in different parts of the world are connected through a mere internet connection. Amidst the information revolution m ass media has become such a massive part of our lives (2018). Mass media is a major source of information for the majority of population in most countries. It can shape public opinion and ensure popular support of particular politicians and policies. As a result, often politicians and other interested parties have incentives to influence the media to make sure it is friendly enough, whenever they have opportunity to do so. The main goal of this paper is to overview evidence on the effect of mass media on people's behavior, primarily, in the political domain. However, since the influence of mass media provides incentives for politicians and other agents to influence media coverage, we will also discuss evidence of media capture and the impact of captured media. This *Opuscle* reviews the recent economic literature on the effects of mass media. We start with briefly describing theoretical framework for analyzing the effect of mass media. We then discuss the challenges of estimating media effects, and review papers that quantify media impact in various circumstances. Finally, we'll talk about the evidence for media capture and the limits of media captures. 2011). such effects take place if media omits some relevant facts or provides deliberately incomplete information. In these instances even fully rational Bayesian media consumers that are aware that the media is biased cannot fully undo the bias without getting access to more complete information from alternative sources. Therefore, biased media can have an effect on people's behavior even in the situations when the audience knows about a potential bias in media reports (see Strömberg 2016, Prat 2016, and Gentzkow, Shapiro, and Stone 2016 for more detailed surveys of the theoretical literature on biased media).

India's internet users expected to register double digit growth to reach 627 million in 2019, driven by rapid internet growth in rural areas, market research agency Kantar IMRB Wednesday said. In its ICUBE 2018 report that tracks digital adoption and usage trends in India, it noted that the number of internet users in India has registered an annual growth of 18 percent and is estimated at 566 million as of December 2018, a 40 percent overall internet penetration, it observed. Of the total user base, 87 percent or 493 million Indians, are defined as regular users, having accessed internet in last 30 days. Nearly 293 million active internet users reside in urban India, while there are 200 million active users in rural India, it said. The report found that 97 percent of users use mobile phone as one of the devices to access internet. While internet users grew by 7 percent in urban India, reaching 315 million users in 2018, digital adoption is now being propelled by rural India, registering a 35 percent growth in internet users over the past year. It is now estimated that there are 251 million internet users in rural India, and this is expected to reach 290 million by the end of 2019, the report said. Increased availability of bandwidth, cheap data plans and increased awareness driven by government programmes seem to have rapidly bridged the digital gap between urban and rural India. Consequently, the penetration in rural India has increased from 9 per cent in 2015 to 25 percent in 2018," it added. Bihar registered the highest growth in internet users across both urban and rural areas, registering a growth of 35 percent over last year. The report also noted that the internet usage is more gender balanced than ever before with women comprising 42 percent of total internet users. (Report - The Economic Times, 2019).

The Indian Readership Survey (IRS) data released for Q1 of 2019 reveals that the overall readership of newspapers has grown from 407 million readers in 2017 to 425 million readers at the end of the first quarter of 2019. The report was released by the Media Research Users Council (MRUC) on Friday. While Hindi and regional dailies grew at 3.9 per cent and 5.7 per cent, respectively, English newspapers saw a 10.7 per cent growth, though on a small base. Hindi dailies had 186 million readers, while regional readership stood at 211 million in IRS Q1 2019. English newspaper readership went up from 28 million to 31 million between the 2017 and Q1 2019 surveys. Total readership of magazines was up 9 million to 87 million, according to the latest IRS data, while business dailies too reported a healthy growth. The report is based on a rolling average of the data from last three quarters of IRS 2017 and one fresh quarter from IRS 2019. The sample size for the latest IRS was 324,286 households. The consumption of online newspapers also saw growth. In IRS 2017, 4 per cent of the total universe consumed online newspapers, while in IRS 2019 the number has grown to 5 per cent. The growth is led by New Consumer Classification System A1 where 27 per cent of the total universe consumed online newspapers. In consumption, the clear outlier was digital as the percentage of people who accessed the internet grew from 19 per cent of the total universe to 24 per cent. TV, radio and magazine consumption showed marginal increase, while newspaper readership and cinema consumption remained flat. However, since the universe of media consumption itself grew, there was growth in newspaper and cinema consumption in absolute numbers. Internet penetration stood at 36 per cent, with urban markets seeing penetration in excess of 50 per cent, and rural markets at 28 per cent. However, in terms of absolute numbers, 50 per cent of internet users came from rural areas. Vikram Sakhuja, group CEO, Madison Media & OOH, Madison World, and IRS technical committee chairman, said, "Overall media consumption, and print in particular, is vibrant and growing. Most stakeholders should be encouraged with this snapshot of how India is consuming media and print. A number of newspapers and periodicals are published in Hindi, English, and Urdu. The Pioneer was founded in Allahabad in 1865 by George Allen. Amar Ujala, Dainik Bhaskar, Dainik Jagran, Rajasthan Patrika and Hindustan Dainik have a wide circulation, with local editions published from several important cities. Major English language newspapers which are published and sold in large numbers are The Telegraph, The Times of India, Hindustan Times, The Hindu, The Statesman, The Indian Express, and Asian Age. Some prominent financial dailies like The Economic Times, Financial Express, Business Line, and Business Standard are widely circulated. Vernacular newspapers such as those in Hindi, Nepali, Gujarati, Odia, Urdu, and Punjabi are also read by a select readership. Doordarshan is the state-owned television broadcaster. Multi system operators provide a mix of Hindi, English, Bengali, Nepali and international channels via cable. Hindi 24-hour television news channels are NDTV India, DD News, Zee News, Aaj Tak, News18 India, and ABP News. All India Radio is a public radio station. There are 32 private FM stations available in major cities like Lucknow, Kanpur, Varanasi, Allahabad, Agra, and Noida. Cell phone providers include Vodafone, Airtel, BSNL, Reliance Jio, Reliance Communications, Telenor, Aircel, Tata Indicom, Idea Cellular, and Tata DoCoMo. Broadband internet is available in select towns and cities and is provided by the state-run BSNL and by private companies. Dial-up access is provided throughout the state by BSNL and other providers.

Indian Media consist of several different types of communications: television, radio, cinema, newspapers, magazines, and Internet-based Web sites/portals. Indian media was active since the late 18th century with print media started in 1780, radio broadcasting initiated in 1927, and the screening of Auguste and Louis Lumière moving pictures in Bombay initiated during the July of 1895. It is among the oldest and largest media of the world. Media in India has been free and independent throughout most of its history, even before establishment of Indian empire by Ashoka the Great on the foundation of righteousness, openness, morality and spirituality. The period of emergency (1975–1977), declared by Prime Minister Indira Gandhi, was the brief period when India's media was faced with potential government retribution. The country consumed 99 million newspaper copies as of 2007-making it the second largest market in the world for newspapers. By 2009, India had a total of 81,000,000 Internet users-comprising 7.0% of the country's population, and 7,570,000 people in India also had access to broadband Internet as of 2010 - making it the 11th largest country in the world in terms of broadband Internet users. As of 2009, India is among the 4th largest television broadcast stations in the world with nearly 1,400 stations. Snapshot of evolution of media in India is as below. Mass media in India - Bengal: The Bengal Gazette was started by James Augustus Hicky in 1780. The Gazette, a two-sheet newspaper, specialised in writing on the private lives of the Sahibs of the Company. He dared even to mount scurrillious attacks on the Governor-General, Warren Hastings', wife, which soon landed "the late printer to the Honourable Company" in trouble. Hicky was sentenced to a 4 months jail term and Rs.500 fine, which did not deter him. After a bitter attack on the Governor-General and the Chief Justice, Hicky was sentenced to one year in prison and fined Rs.5,000, which finally drove him to penury.

Introduction

These were the first tentative steps of journalism in India. Mass media in India - Calcutta: B.Messink and Peter Reed were pliant publishers of the India Gazette, unlike their infamous predecessor.

The colonial establishment started the Calcutta Gazette. It was followed by another private initiative the Bengal Journal. The Oriental Magazine of Calcutta Amusement, a monthly magazine made it four weekly newspapers and one monthly magazine published from Calcutta, now Kolkata. Mass media in India - Madras Chennai: The Madras Courier was started in 1785 in the southern stronghold of Madras, which is now called Chennai. Richard Johnson, its founder, was a government printer. Madras got its second newspaper when, in 1791, Hugh Boyd, who was the editor of the Courier quit and founded the Hurkaru. Tragically for the paper, it ceased publication when Boyd passed away within a year of its founding. It was only in 1795 that competitors to the Courier emerged with the founding of the Madras Gazette followed by the India Herald. The latter was an "unauthorised" publication, which led to the deportation of its founder Humphreys. The Madras Courier was designated the purveyor of official information in the Presidency. In 1878, The Hindu was founded, and played a vital role in promoting the cause of Indian independence from the colonial yoke. It's founder, Kasturi Ranga Iyengar, was a lawyer, and his son, K Srinivasan assumed editorship of this pioneering newspaper during for the first half of the 20th century.

Today this paper enjoys the highest circulation in South India, and is among the top five nationally. Mass media in India - Bombay: Bombay, now Mumbai, surprisingly was a late starter - The Bombay Herald came into existence in 1789. Significantly, a year later a paper called the Courier started carrying advertisements in Gujarati. The first media merger of sorts: The Bombay Gazette, which was started in 1791, merged with the Bombay Herald the following year. Like the Madras Courier, this new entity was recognised as the publication to carry "official notifications and advertisements". 'A Chronicle of Media and the State', by Jeebesh Bagchi in the Sarai Reader 2001 is a handy timeline on the role of the state in the development of media in India for more than a century. Bagchi divides the timeline into three 'ages'. The Age of Formulation, which starts with the Indian Telegraph Act in 1885 and ends with the Report of the Sub-Committee on Communication, National Planning Committee in 1948. State of Modern Mass Media: After Independence, the Indian media had evolved, realigned and reinvented itself to a large extent, and now-a-days you can see a clear division between commercial and aesthetic expressions of our Media Giants, sometimes arbitrary. Modern mass communication media is poles apart relative to any aesthetic feeling: vulgarity and arrogance nullify any hypothesis of meaning. Aesthetics is the more powerful answer to violence of modern mass communication.

Today's mass communication media seems to elude every determination, exposing its message to all possible variants, it finishes to abolish it. Goal of mass communication is always the unbiased dissipation of any content, and the World Wide Web is no exception, and surely is the most efficient media tool. It's also very interesting to observe how the old media are becoming more and more permeable to blogs and D.I.Y. information. This phenomenon is not due to a fascination in more democratic information sources. On the contrary - the pressure is rising due to the growth of the eyes' (cameras and new digital devices) that are watching the same events that mainstream media are reporting to us: the possibility of being uncovered are too many and broadcast journalists are forced to tell the truth (or at least a plausible version of it). As a consequence, blogs have become the major source of news and information about many global affairs. We also have to consider that bloggers are often the only real journalists, as they (at their own risk) provide independent news in countries where the mainstream media is censored, biased or under control (nimc-india.com 2018).

In the previous sections, we focused mainly on the effects of mass media on political outcomes. However, the effects of media exposure are not limited to political domain and can be manifested in a variety of other areas ranging from education to fertility decisions. Some recent papers look at the effect of media exposure on education. Theoretically, the effect of TV on education is ambiguous. On the one hand, as long as TV programs contain useful information that is presented in a rich language, watching such programs can improve knowledge and increase language proficiency. On the other hand, watching TV can crowd out more useful activities such as reading, studying, social interactions etc., and, thus, have a negative effect on individuals' development, especially for young children. Thus, whether the effect of TV on educations is positive or negative is ultimately an empirical question. Gentzkow and Shapirob (2008) used the difference-in-differences approach, described above, to estimate the effect of TV exposure in early childhood on educational outcomes of young adults. In particular, they exploited the fact that television children's cognitive abilities (Durante et al 2016, Hernæs et al 2016). Television can also affect family outcomes, such as fertility and family planning by exposing the viewers to particular role models their entertainment content.

Facebook :- This is the largest social media network on the Internet, both in terms of total number of users and name recognition. Facebook came into existence on February 4, 2004, Facebook has within 12 years managed to collect more than 1.59 billion monthly active users and this automatically makes it one of the best mediums for connecting people from all over the world with your business. It is predictable that more than 1 million small and medium-sized businesses use the platform to advertise their business (S.Shabnoor,S.Tajinder, 2016).

Twitter:- We might be thinking that restrictive our posts to 140 characters is no way to advertise our business, but we will be shocked to know that this social media stage has more than 320 million active monthly users who can build use of the 140 character limit to pass on information. Businesses can use Twitter to interact with prospective clients, answer questions, release latest news and at the same time use the targeted ads with specific audiences. Twitter was founded on March 21, 2006, and has its headquarters in San Francisco, California (Shabnoor, S. & Tajinder, S. 2016).

Google+ :- Google+ is one of the popular social media sites in these days. Its SEO value alone makes it a must-use tool for any small business. Google+ was propelled on December 15, 2011, and has joined the major alliances enlisting 418 dynamic million clients as of December 2015.

YouTube :- YouTube: the biggest and most well known video-based online networking site — was established on February 14, 2005, by three previous PayPal workers. It was later purchased by Google in November 2006 for $1.65 billion. YouTube has more than 1 billion site guests for every month and is the second most well known internet searcher behind Google (Bin Zhao et al., 2011).

Instagram:- Instagram is a visual online networking stage. The site has more than 400 million dynamic clients and is possessed by Facebook. A significant number of its clients utilize it to post data about travel, form, sustenance, workmanship and comparable subjects. The stage is likewise recognized by its remarkable channels together with video and photograph altering highlights. Right around 95 percent of Instagram clients additionally utilize Facebook (Mahmoudi Sidi Ahmed et al., 2008).

WhatsApp:- WhatsApp Messenger is a cross-platform instant messaging client for smartphones, PCs and tablets. This application needs Internet connection to send images, texts, documents, audio and video messages to other users that have the app installed on their devices. Launched in January 2010, WhatsApp Inc. was purchased by Facebook on February 19, 2004, for about $19.3 billion. Today, more than 1 billion persons make use of the administration to speak with their companions, friends and family and even clients (Nagar *et al.,*).

BizSugar:- BizSugar is a person to person communication stage and specialty asset for entrepreneurs, business visionaries and directors. The site was made in 2007 by DBH Communications, Inc., a supplier of honor winning business distributions, and later obtained by Small Business Trends LLC, in 2009. The stage enables clients to share recordings, articles, blog entries, podcast among other substance. It additionally enables clients to view and vote on entries by different individuals (Bin Zhao et al., 2011).

Flickr:- Flickr, articulated "Glint," is an online picture and video facilitating stage that was made by the then Vancouver-construct Ludicorp in light of February 10, 2004, and later obtained by Yahoo in 2005. The stage is well known with clients who share and install photos. Flickr had more than 112 million clients and had its impression in more than 63 nations. Million of photographs are shared day by day on Flickr (Nagar *et a.,*).

Tumblr:- Tumblr is a standout amongst the most hard to utilize informal communication stages, but at the same time it's a standout amongst the most fascinating locales. The stage permits a few diverse post groups, including cite posts, talk posts, video and photograph posts and in addition sound posts, so you are never constrained in the kind of substance that you can share.[4] Like Twitter, reblogging, which is more similar to retweeting, is speedy and simple. The long range informal communication site was established by David Karp in February 2007 and at present has more than 200 million sites (Bin Zhao et al., 2011).

Social media is composed of those interactive platforms on the internet, which may be web or mobile-based, that involve user-generated content and their main pur-pose is social interaction. They often gather people who share common interests. It is essential that these pages are interactive; the interaction is bi- or multidirectional. Characteristically the communication on these websites happens as individual people. Social media is an umbrella term that consists of various types of social media. In some cases it may be difficult to determine whether a website, application or plat-form fits the definition of social media or not. Often the word social media is used synonymously with online social networks to refer to websites such as Facebook, Google+ and Linked in. However, the extensive concept of social media also includes other types, such as blogging, micro-blogging, online rating, social news, social bookmarking, forum, and various multimedia plat-forms. Social networks are web-based applications or platforms that allow communication between users, which may be through information, comments, messages, images or other types of communication (Oxford Dictionaries 2016a). Social networks include websites like Facebook, Google+ and LinkedIn, and usually user profiles are a key part of the platform (Cite 2012).

Traditional media consists of media such as television, print, radio, direct mail and outdoor, which are conventional forms of advertising (Quilici, 2011). Advertising in traditional media involves many challenges including the large amount of valueless contacts, high expenses, and the diminishing impact related to the changes of media behavior and the digital revolution (Karjaluoto 2010). States that the social media sites encourage negative behaviors for teen students such as procrastination (catching up with friends), and they are more likely to drink and drug. However, every day, many students are spending countless hours immersed in social media, such as Facebook, MySpace, World of Warcraft, or Sim City. At first glance this may seem like a waste of time; however it also helps students to develop important knowledge and social skills, and be active citizens who create and share content. At present, whether social media is favorable or unfavorable, many students utilize these sites on a daily basis.

As social media sites continue to grow in popularity it is our belief that technology is a vital part of today's student success equation. Many researchers have been diving into a considerable amount of research on how social media influences student retention at colleges. Many parents are worried that their college students are spending too much time on Facebook and other social media sites and not enough time studying. Therefore, our research ascertains the relationship between the social media and students' study efficiency. Schill (2011). Traditional media relies on a one-to-many model. The brand message is created and communicated to a mass audience through traditional media channels, as a one-way communication. This one-way communication is not as effective in creating engagement or promoting word of mouth, in comparison to social media. (Hausman, 2014). Ma and Chan (2014) buttress that social networks, especially Twitter and Facebook are becoming exceptionally popular platforms of sharing millions of videos, phrases, photos, audios, and articles. Studies on the preferred social media platform have established that Whatsapp remains the most popular social media application. A Ghanian study found that the majority of students used WhatsApp as the most widely used social media platform followed by Facebook and tweeter (Mingle & Adams, 2015). This finding was confirmed by Ogaji et al. (2017) who sampled Kenyan students. More than half of the sampled undergraduate students at the University of Brunei Darusalam reported that they would still continue to use whatsapp even if it was no longer freely avaliable (Ahad & Lim, 2014). Consistent with research conducted by Mingle & Adams (2015) and confirmed by Ogaji et al. (2017) and Ahad & Lim (2014), the current study found that most of the students used WhatsApp as the most widely used social media platform followed by Facebook and tweeter. Ahad & Lim (2014) are among those who provide the reason why students use whatspp. They argue that built as an alternative to short messaging service (SMS), Whatsapp offers real-time texting or communication, including the ease of sharing information (e.g. contact list) or media content (e.g. audio, video files, images, location data). Although Whatsapp seems to be popular, Young and Rogers (1998) argue that interactive featuresof the internet such as chat rooms are the most addictive.

A social media is an online platform which people use to build social networks or social relations with other people who share similar personal or career interests, activities, backgrounds or real-life connections. The impact of social networks on young people is significant. It is becoming increasingly clear that social networks have become part of people's lives. Many adolescent people are using their laptops, tablet computers and smart phones to check Tweets and status updates from their friends and family. Due to the advancement in technology, people are pressured to accept different lifestyles. Social networking sites can assist young people to become more socially capable. Social media is a web-based form of data communication. Social media platforms allow users to have conversations, share information and create web content. Social media has different forms, together with blogs, micro-blogs, wikis, social networking sites, photo-sharing sites, instant messaging, video-sharing sites, podcasts, widgets, virtual worlds, and more. Billions of people around the world use social media to share information and make connections (Mahmoudi Sidi Ahmed et al., 2008).

Social Media is the new buzz sector in promoting that incorporates business, associations and brands which make news, influence companions, to make relations and make groups. Business utilize web-based social networking to upgrade an association's execution in different ways, for example, to achieve business targets, expanding yearly offers of the association. Web-based social networking gives the advantage as a correspondence stage that encourages two way communications between an organization and their stock holders. Business can be advanced through different long range informal communication destinations. A considerable group of the organization advances their business by giving promotion on the online networking with a specific end goal to draw in greatest clients. Clients can associate and collaborate with business on a more individual level by utilizing online networking. Many organizations with the use of social media can make their strategy to promote their Business (Willium .S, 2012).

It is assumed, and to an extent proven, that students are one of the largest segments of Internet users in India. According to a study released in 2010 by Boston Consulting group, there are currently 81 million Internet users in India. As per the report, India is in third place in Asia and fourth place in the world in number of Internet users. India has around 13% of Internet users in Asia and 7.36% in comparison to the world, even though only 5.3% of the Indian population is using the Internet. The majority of Internet users in India fall under the age group of (19-40). Though there is more Internet usage in the major cities of India, Internet penetration into rural areas has also increased. Internet in India is mainly used for e-mailing (95%), job searching (73%), chatting (62%), social networking (51%), while the exception is the visit to websites related to mathematics (48%) (The Boston Consulting Group, The Internet's New Billion, 2010.)

A majority (84%) of internet users are either very or fairly confident that they can recognise advertising online. However, when shown an example of the results returned by Google for a particular online search and with their attention drawn to the adverts that appeared in these results, just half of adults (48%) only gave the correct response by identifying them as sponsored links, despite their being distinguished by a box with the word 'Ad' in it. More than half of internet users (56%) are aware of personalized advertising, in that they are aware that other people might see adverts that are different to those they see. More than one in four internet users (27%) state that everyone would see the same adverts, with 17% unsure. Awareness is lower for internet users aged 65-74 (40%) and 75+ (28%). Users of video-sharing sites were prompted with a list of possible reasons why vloggers might endorse a product. Seven in ten users (72%) were aware that vloggers might be paid by a company to say favorable things about a product or brand, and 28% did not select this option, of whom 12% were unsure. This echoes concerns raised in the qualitative study; some participants felt it wasn't always easy to tell when a YouTuber or social media celebrity was being paid to endorse products.(Adults' Media Use and Attitudes – Report 2017)

Globally, online social media defined as web-based tools that allow users to interact with each other in some wayby sharing information, opinions, knowledge and interests online (Ford & Ravansari, 2017), is shaping human interactions in varied ways. It has been estimated that 94% of adults worldwide own a social media site account and have visited or used one within the last month (Chaffey, 2016). Approximately 73% of adolescents use social media (Lenhart et al.,2010).There is general consensus that one of the most popular Internet activities among college students is social media use as confirmed by Smith & Caruso (2010)who found that 90% of 36,950 university students drawn from 126 U.S.A and Canadian universities use social networking websites.Young people are active social media users (Rideout, Foehr, & Roberts, 2010).

The success of agricultural development programmes in developing countries largely depends on the nature and extent of use of mass media in mobilization of people for development. The planners in developing countries realize that the development of agriculture could be hastened with the effective use of mass media. Radio,Television have been acclaimed to be the most effective media for diffusing the scientific knowledge to the masses. In a country like India, where literacy level is low, the choice of communication media is of vital importance. In this regard the television and radio are significant, as they transfer modern agricultural technology to literate and illiterate farmers alike even in interior areas, within short time. In India farm and home broadcast with agricultural thrust were introduced in 1966, to enlighten farmers on the use of various technologies to boost agricultural development. At present, there are about 50 such radio units all over the country. With the main stream of Indian population engaged actively in agriculture, television could serve as a suitable medium of dissemination of farm information and latest technical know – how. The farmers can easily understand the operations, technology and instruction through television.

In this context, there is an urgent need to explore the socio-economic impact of mass media utilization in India. This study will help us understand mass media utilization pattern, their socio-economic impact and the challenges faced in rural areas. It will also help policymakers, mass media operators, researchers and technology transfer specialists frame development strategies in the future. Hence, present study entitled, **"Study on mass media utilization pattern of the Post Graduate students of agriculture in State Agriculture Universities of Uttar Pradesh."** Has been undertaken with the following objectives:

1. To study the socio-economic profile of students.
2. To study the knowledge extent of students about mass media.
3. To study the utilization pattern of mass media by the students.
4. To find out the relationship between independents variable with those of dependents variable.
5. To assess the constraints in utilization of mass media by the students and suggestions to overcome the constraints.

Importance and justification of the problem:

The aim of the study is to understand the origin and evaluation of the post graduate students' agricultural-based uses of mass media utilization pattern and the impact of these on sustainable livelihoods activities in developing post graduate students of agriculture. Another aspect of this study is to further the understanding of the mass media utilization pattern needs of those involved in communication activities that are instrumental in establishing sustainable livelihoods in developing countries students. Using a qualitative approach through in-depth interviews, this study sought to discover post graduate students' agricultural-based uses of mass media utilization pattern including where the use came from, how the use has been adapted to fit local needs, and how the use is being diffused throughout developing post graduate students of agriculture State Agriculture Universities of Uttar Pradesh, namely the Acharya Narendera Deva University of Agriculture & Technology, Kumargunj, Ayodhya,. So it will be collect the required information from Acharya Narendera Deva University of Agriculture & Technology, Kumargunj, Ayodhya, Chandera Shekhar Azad University of Agriculture & Technology, Kanpur, Sardar vallabhbhai Patel University of Agriculture & technology, Meerut and Banda University of Agriculture & Technology, Banda, in India.

The study is justified because of its approach to trace out the constraints in level of satisfaction of post graduate agriculture students, as to bridge-up the gape and thus, encourage the level of satisfaction of related to mass media utilization pattern development. This would be conducive to planners, administrators, extension workers to do the sincere effort in promotion of awareness and level of satisfaction in communication technology.

The findings of this are expected to provide deeper insights into the utility of mass media utilization pattern adoption and to further examine the function of mass media utilization pattern in the development and growth of post graduate students of agriculture within a developing country.

The results of this study can be useful to national and international initiatives focusing on the role of mass media utilization pattern for development. New application and techniques that will tap the fullest potential of mass media utilization pattern in developing regions of the world may be identified. A local focus brings a unique perspective that will provide greater nuances to students understanding of the amplifications of mass media communication technology to assist in the achievement of development initiatives.

Limitations of the study:

The research studies in social science practically face some limitations and the same is with the present study. Despite the various uses of mass media utilization pattern in post graduate students of agriculture, there is also limitation related with its use. The study has following limitations-

1. Concerning the sample size selection of post graduate students of agriculture in study local areas, was the problem, because of its large size, owing to this,

investigator has selected sample from only college of agriculture all selected State Agriculture Universities
2. On account of time limitation, the investigator has selected only post graduate students of agriculture.
3. As the entire investigation was based on the individuals perceptions and expressed opinion of the under study.

Chapter-II
REVIEW OF LITERATURE

In any scientific investigation a comprehensive review of literature is an essential part. Plays important role and it guides the research work for their research work and acquaint them with the earlier work done in the related fields. In addition it also provides basis for developing a theoretical framework and deriving hypothesis.

In any scientific investigation, a comprehensive and relevant review of illustrate is very important. Only a few research work have been conducted in the preview of the proposition undertaken for the study have been collected and are being summaries below in chronological sequence. There are various studies which have some bearing directly on the present study are being abstract under appropriate heading as follows:

1. Socio-economic profile of students.
2. Knowledge extent of students about mass media.
3. Utilization pattern of mass media by the students.
4. Relationship between independents variable with those of dependents variable.
5. Constraints in utilization of mass media by the students and suggestions to overcome the constraints.

2.1 Socio-economic profile of students:

Josephson (1987) randomly assigned 7 to 9 year-old boys to watch either a violent or am nonviolent film before they played a game of floor hockey in school. He found that for aggressive boys (those who scored above average on a measure of aggressiveness), the combination of seeing a violent film and movie- associated cue stimulated significantly more assaultive behavior than any other combination of film and cue.

Gupta (1992) calculate the maximum number of respondents preferred the radio listening (73.33%), than reading the newspapers (66.67%) and television viewing (60.00%).

Review of Literature

Rao and Raghavan (1996) surveyed the origin and the initial role as well as the post-independence growth of each of the mass media as part of the country's developing political economy. The book also presents the findings of the first ever country wide in depth study of the social effects of the mass media. The book discusses the impact of media on education and awareness of common people. The suggestions are also given for development of media to improve the society.

Huesmann and Taylor (2003) calculate that cable systems, videocassette recorders, and video games have increased exposure. Hand-held cameras and video monitors now permit filming of actual crimes in progress. Economic competition for viewers, particularly young viewers, has placed a premium on media depictions of violence. Not long after the introduction of television in American households, there occurred a dramatic increase in violent crime.

Mbugua (2004) calculate that although family conflict and jealousy are frequently portrayed on prime-time television, the portrayals are not predominantly antisocial.

Baym *et al* (2004) studied social interactions of college students across all media. Their results indicated that 64% still prefer face-to-face interaction, 18.4% prefer the telephone, and only 16.1% prefer the internet for making social contacts.

Lohar and Kumbar (2008) the impact of the resources on the student academic work/study. Also describes the problems faced in using the electronic resources. Hence a survey of 110 undergraduate and postgraduate (BE) students of different disciplines was conducted tlirougli questionnaire. Finally, it is concluded that the main intention using CD-ROM and INTERNET resources and services has been the academic interest of the student community.

Pempek *et al.* (2009) calculate that facebook is used an average of 27 minutes per day by college students. "Facebook provides colleges with a simple way to engage students with informal conversations, build community, and easily view prospective students' public activities and interests for recruitment and admissions efforts." Students use Facebook 84% of the time to communicate with their friends through these features primarily between 9 p.m. and midnight.

Shao (2009) found that the three video-website usage behaviors of the model are consuming, participating, and producing. Consuming behaviors refer to the individuals who only watch, read, or view for information and entertainment. Participating behaviors include both user-to-user interaction and user-to-content interaction (such as scoring, adding to a playlist, sharing, commenting), primarily for social interaction and community development. Producing behaviors refers to the creation and publication of one's personal work such as text, images, audio, and video, mainly based on self expression or self-actualization motivations.

Giffords (2009) calculate the more effects of the sexual content in 4 kinds of media adolescents use frequently, television, music, movies, and magazines, on black and white adolescents' sexual behavior. The few studies of the effects of television on adolescents' sexual beliefs havefound that prime-time programs and music videos focusing on sex outside marriage promote more permissive attitudes about premarital sex.

Hillary (2010) examined the depiction of conflict, jealousy, envy, and rivalry in family interactions in prime-time network programs. The data showed that more than 30% of the conflict situations involved parents and children, 19% involved spouses, and 13% involved siblings. Integrative strategies, considered to be the most healthy were used most by mothers and sons, and more destructive strategies were used by siblings and spouses.

Lenhart *et al.* (2010) found that 71% of young adults have a Facebook account. The current study indicated that Facebook and e-mail were the social network websites of choice, with 99% of college students using Facebook and 90% using e-mail.

Kakade and Raut (2012) calculate mass Media contributes largely towards empowerment of education in the society. The Mass Media play pivotal role in promoting education in India. It is clear and confirmed that our day to day life is influenced by the Mass Media. Newspaper, Radio, Television, Cinema, Internet etc., have outgrown themselves from mass communicator to influence our day to day activities and are leaving deep imprint on our attitude, conduct and ideologies. Mass Media is a prime resource in achieving the goal in socio-economical and cultural sectors and also for the development of education. Thus, Mass Media is providing formal and informal education. Many researchers have confirmed the fact that Mass Media have really helped the people in getting proper education.

Tanwar and Priyanka (2016) examined most children witness some form of media violence almost every day, whether on the news, in a cartoon, on the Internet, in a TV show or in a movie. These exposures, whether short-term or long-term, can result in negative psychological effects, including increased aggressive behavior and a diminished level of excitement toward violent acts. New longitudinal studies with larger samples are needed to estimate accurately how much habitual childhood exposure to media violence increases the risk for extreme violence.

Trivedi (2016) defined intention as be state of mind directing a person's attention (and therefore experience and action) toward a specific object (goal) or a path in order to achieve something (means)" (p. 442). Past studies have provided much needed empirical evidences about entrepreneurial intention among students from multiple perspectives.

Balaji and Ragavan (2016) revealed that the findings of the study indicate that the information seeking behavior of faculty and research scholars are varied. The large libraries will depend on the strength of the collections and available online resources to facilitate the easy access to the information. The library staff must aware how the faculty and research scholar will seek the information and their needs. The reference librarian should help the users in locating the information and their by help the faculty and scholars to improve the seeking behavior and find the needs of the users of the library.

Singh *et al.* (2017) found that the effect maximum number of the respondents (57.33%) was observed in the category of 22 to 26 years of age. The all students/respondents were found in the B.Sc. agriculture in (41.33 %), M.Sc. (42.34 %) and Ph.D. students in (16 %) respectively. The little less than half of the respondents

(48.33%) belonged to backward categories of caste followed by (29.67 %) General caste and (22.00 %) Scheduled caste respectively. The maximum number of the respondents was observed unmarried (93%). It is apparent from the highest number of respondents (69.34%) was found having medium level of economic motivation, while (18.33%) and (12.33%) respondents were such who had high and low levels of economic motivation, respectively.

Treapat (2017) observeded that using the media channels the influence upon the youth's attitude and behavior concerns that 56% do not consider that they are dramatically influenced by the information received through such means, so that it produce an attitude or behaviour change. The weight for the response „In a big proportion" is of only 8% for this question, aspect that is not bad at all as, also considering the conclusions that were drawn for the previous questions, the manipulation, the entertainment and the irrelevant information are not a proper base for changing the behaviour but only for those who do not have enough life experience to judge/separate the good from the evil. If the slight change of the 56% of the respondents will be towards choosing the real sources of culture, towards avoiding manipulation and towards education, then the change is beneficial and we can state that the mass-media influence is also desirable.

Kumar and Maurya (2018) calculate that mass media regular happenings and events around us educate us, in one or the other way. It would not be an exaggeration to say that the existence of human beings is fruitless without education. An educated person has the ability to change the world, as he/she is brimming with confidence and assured of making the right moves. It Makes Better Citizens, Ensures A Productive Future, Opens New Vistas, Spreads Awareness, Helps In Decision-Making, Bolsters Confidence.

2.2 Knowledge extent of students about mass media:

Ajzen (1991) showed that the opinion of important reference groups such as parents, spouse, friends, and relatives may also influence the behavior of a person to perform or not perform certain actions. In the past, it was found that a social norm has a very weak influence on entrepreneurial intention.

Tadasad and Metasheela (2001) calculate that the studied two hundred and four postgraduate students of Gulbarga University. The study reveals that books, newspapers, popular magazines, class notes, notes of seniors, are the most useful sources of information. General dictionaries, subject dictionaries, subject encyclopedia and scientific periodicals are also useful sources of information for the PG students. Memoranda, diaries and letters, CD databases, /dissertation, microforms, course material of open universities, geographical sources, directories, manuals, research reports are never used by a majority of PG-students.

Inamdar and Rotti (2004) calculate that the computer knowledge was higher among postgraduates (93.3%) than undergraduates (84.5%). Student learned computers by self-learning, attending classes and using manuals. Writing letters was the most common use of the computer (post graduates, 100%; undergraduates, 87.5%). 71% of the post graduates and 43% of the undergraduates used English language dictionaries. About 61% of the undergraduates used computers for playing games. Students also used computer for watching movies. MS Office was the most commonly used software (postgraduates, 100%; undergraduates, 72.2%).

Spitzberg (2006) calculate a model of CMC competence similar to earlier views of interpersonal communication competence, where competence is determined by the motivation, knowledge, and skills of the interact ant in relation to the demands of the context and desired outcomes of the discourse. One important element in self-presentation is self-disclosure because it allows an individual some ability to shape and control self relevant knowledge. Communication competence plays a significant role in how one engages in self-presentation.

Quan-Haase and Young (2010) calculate that majority of college students visited their social networking sites several times a day, and this shows that the extent of usage of social media sites is frequent. Several reasons were given as to why college students were using social networking websites. The most important reason given was to communicate with family and friends. Entertainment and boredom were also prominent reasons for use social networking sites.

Sinha (2012) assumed on the extent of internet awareness and status on use of e-resources by the Assam University Library users. The period of survey was July to August 2008 covering the users comprising of faculty, research scholars, UG/PG students and other staff using internet accessing to the e-resources under the UGCINFONET Digital Library Consortium. The data is analyzed using software. The paper highlights the findings in respect of Internet Awareness, its use pattern and attitude of library users towards the electronic resources, in this context.

Olowu and Fasola (2012) revealed that majority of the students in tertiary institutions in Oyo State affirmed that they spend more time on social media and that they felt agitated when they are not able to access their social network at least twice daily. This established a high level of social media addiction among the students.

Leiserowitz and Thaker (2012) conclude that a large majority of the respondents, nearly

70 percent of them were in favor of a country- wide programmed to teach Indians about global warming in their educational institutions. Apart from this, a majority of the respondents said that policies have to be incorporated immediately so as to reduce wasteful use of energy, water and fuel even if these measures may lead to price rise.

Ndaku (2013) indicated that, 92.3% was aware of social media and 96.2% had access to the internet. Similarly, majority (46.1%) used their mobile phones to access the internet and Facebook was very popular among the respondents.

Jogan and Sushma (2015) examined the views of postgraduate students' on the access, awareness and usage in facilitating their research and their satisfaction with the sources and services currently provided. It suggested further for an improvement in the access facilities with high Internet speed and subscription to more e-resources by the University Library. The study attempted to encounter different problems faced by the students during accessing e-resources.

Aramide *et al.* (2015) calculate the facebook (751 or 90.2%) and Twitter (646 or 77.6%) were the most commonly accessible social media networks while meeting with friends (651 or 78.2%), getting news (566 or 67.9%), communication (554 or 66.5%) and online learning (450 or 54.0%) were major purposes for social media usage among the undergraduate students. Low level of social media addiction and positive self-perception were also established among the undergraduate students.

Bharadwaja and Sharma (2017) examined extent of utilization of different media as source of information exchange. Among the traditional media, majority used news paper daily (90.00%), magazines daily (83.30%), radio/FM daily (72.00%) and television daily (94.65%). Further it could be noticed that extent of utilization of different mass media (based on total score) in the rank order of Television, News paper, Magazines and Radio/FM. Among the digital mass media, Internet surfing (97.30%), E-mail (76.65%), Face book (70.60%), what's App (86.60%), Hike (53.30%), Telegram (43.30%) and Skype (30.65%) were used daily as a source of information by majority of students.

Chohda and Gupta (2017) found that 70 per cent are aware about the e-journals and databases. The result indicated that both print and electronic e-journals are highly preferred by students but access them in other places then departmental library and 32.22 per cent respondents spent time more than hours for internet access. The study will be useful for the academic librarians in improving the shortcomings of their institutes and will procure the required e-journals for their Institutes.

Chandran (2018) it was fount four kinds of purposes such as Research, Learning, Current information and Teaching. It was investigated that the utmost 51.53% of the post graduate students used the resources for their research studies, followed by 30.77% of the users who used the resources for learning and current information 15.38%. It was noted that only the minimum number of the respondents (2.30%) used them for teaching purposes.

Wakoli (2018) it was also reported the 57% of the respondents were positive that sexual information from their favorite mass media source makes them desire to have sex?

Review of Literature

However 43% percent of the respondents don't agree that sexual information can make them have desire for sex. Those respondents who were of the opinion noted that by watching pornographic most students feel it's worth to try and put what they have seen into practical. Most of the students (62%) agree that they have at some point watched pornographic movies. Out of the sampled population it is only 30% of the students who do disagree to the view of the majority. Respondent's response on how frequent they use the following media to access sexual information.

2.3 Utilization pattern of mass media by the students:

Bao (1998) findings reported that 40.2% of respondents used the Web on a daily basis, 38.3% weekly, and 10.7% on a monthly basis. About10% respondents said they seldom or never used the Internet. It was also discovered that students and faculty searched the Internet for information related to both their academic (83.2%) and nonacademic studies (73.8%).

Barlow and Gragham (1999) calculate that 96% of the organization which responded, use computers for some aspect of their library and information services, 91% of the sample used various internet facilities including e-mail. World Wide Web, files transfer protocol (FTP) & TELNET.

Biradar and Kumar (2000) calculate impact of personal attributes on use of periodicals. For the present study, the questionnaire method was use to collect necessary data. Result of the study show that large number of teachers and researcher scholars use the subject periodicals most frequently.

Nagireddy and Yakub Ali (2006) calculate that 87% to 90% of the students used Google search engine and 41%to 60% used yahoo. It is also found that 65% to 72% used e-mail for academic purpose, and 49% to 72 % used it for personnel communication regarding e- Journals and CD-ROM databases, 77% of science students,, 76%of social sciences students and 82% of humanities students were accessing the e- Journal. 60% to 75% of all the subject students referred to CD-ROM database. Finally, 84% of science students, 82% of social science students and 94% of humanities students stated that they were satisfied with the staff performance and rated the library services in the IT environment.

Suhail and Bargees (2006) calculate that a great majority of the students (84%) found the Internet helpful for worldwide communication; 78% reported that Internet use actually helped improving their grades; 74% agreed that their reading, writing and information processing skills had expanded by using the Internet. Another 48% reported that they had become better students by using the Internet.

Khare *et al.* (2007) show that the rate of Internet use is more in research scholars of Science, Life Sciences, Engineering, Technology and Management faculties as compared to the faculties of Arts, Social Sciences, Law, Education and Commerce. Among the non-users of Internet, the number of female research scholars is more as compared to male. The research scholars use Internet for research purpose, entertainment as well as for job search.

Nikam and Pramodium (2007) calculate that use of e-journals and databases by the users of University of Mysore. Nearly 200 responses to a survey based on questionnaire have been analyzed and presented. Besides, studying the use of e-journals and databases. The role of information communication of these resources is also discussed.

Boyd and Ellison (2007) calculate that allow users to develop a personal profile, identify other users ("friends") with whom they have a connection, read and react to postings made by other users on the site, and send and receive messages either privately or publicly. Individuals may choose to send private messages, write on other user's walls, organize social activities, and keep informed about other user's daily activities.

Sahu and Mishra (2008) found that Google was the most frequently used search engine (90%), majority of the respondents (55%) used internet for less than 2 hours a week and the basic purpose of using the internet was related to education (64%). The study concluded that free internet service with increasing number of e-journals and e-databases facility is of great importance to meet the emerging needs of the users of university education system.

Sharma (2009) calculate that majority of the teachers 46 (88.46%) and research scholars 28 (93.33%) preferred to use e-Journals, second highest preference was WWW and use of e-Mail with 30 (57.69%) and 41 (78.84%) among teachers whereas 23 (76.66%) and 18 (60.00%) among research scholars. It was also found that 42 (80.77%) teachers and 26 (86.67%) research scholars were able to access the e-Resources very easily and it was also found that 33 (63.46%) teachers and 26 (86.67%) research scholars usually use e-Resources and 15 (28.85%) teachers and 4 (13.33%) research scholars use the e-Resources sometimes and only 4 (7.69%) teachers' use e-Resources rarely. From the study, it was found that use of e-Resources was very common among the teachers and research scholars of the surveyed university and majority of the teachers and research scholars are dependent on e-Resources to get the desired and relevant information. But the practical use of e-Resources was not up to the mark, secondly infrastructure and training programs should also be revised as per the requirements.

Biradar *et al.* (2009) found the 77.22% respondents made daily visits to the library and 15.84% respondents visit library once in two days followed by occasional visits (4.95%). A very small percent of respondents (1.98%) visit the library once in a week. That majority of the students (88.12%) visited the library to read journals and magazines, to borrow books (87.12%), and to read newspapers (67.32%), to prepare assignments (58.41%) and to improve general knowledge (51.48%). The above analysis reveals that the students are more interested in reading books, newspapers and journals. Only 13.86% of students visited the library for recreational purpose and 4.95% respondents visited the library for internet browsing.

Kiragu (2010) calculate that 52.9% low drug users reported low mass media exposure as compared to 9.3% who reported high mass media exposure. For high alcohol and cigarettes users, 58.2% had mass media exposure. This is compared to 4.2% high alcohol and cigarettes users who had low mass media exposure. The results indicated that

15.7% of the respondents had seen or heard pro-alcohol and cigarettes advertisement on the internet.

Kumar and Dominic (2011) calculate that majority of the respondents were satisfied with the books available in the library and these respondents expressed the view that they were more than satisfied with the arrangement of books and services provided by the library. It was also found that 35% of the users only visited the library daily and the rest were not spending much time in the library every week. Hence necessary steps have to be taken to increase the users strength to the library and utilizing the libraryfor more hours.

Hussain (2012) calculate that 90% of the respondents had a Facebook account, LinkedIn, 53%, and Twitter 25%. Majority (92%) used social media for information, 87% for networking, and 76% for learning.

Natarajan (2012) found that most of the students use the library daily and the resources are utilized effectively. Internet is used as the major source of information. The respondents are satisfied with the library facilities and services. Future implications: The study can be further extended to larger number of library users from different management institutions of the country. Social implications: It acts as a guide to the library professionals to educate the users even in digital environment. The types of collection may be increased from local to national and international level in all subjects and as per the discipline. Keywords: Information seeking behaviour, e-journals, OPAC, management institutions, information needs. Paper Type: Survey cum Research

Javed and Bhatti (2013) findings show that the majority of postgraduate students always use general books and were strongly satisfied with this resource. The also frequently use the Internet and most of the respondents use the Internet for educational purposes. Students were also satisfied with the library's reference books collection. Respondents were somewhat satisfied with the periodical collection, and abstract and index services. Knowledge of the different databases supplied by the library and the usage of these databases was unsatisfactory. Students viewed the library as a convenient study place. Respondents pointed out that the slow speed of the Internet and constant electric power failures impeding access to authentic information are the problems they faced while using the Internet.

Ram *et al.* **(2014)** calculate that more than (78.80%) of the respondents were having media utilization, followed by high (12.72%) and low (8.48%) mass media utilization. The possible reason for this could be that the respondents were post –graduate students who hand to use mass media fore different educational purpose respectively.

Upadhyaya (2014) calculate that media-related habits, about 52.21 percent of the students read the *newspapers* for 15 minutes to half an hour daily. As many as 38.36 percent of the students read magazines for less than 15 minutes a daily. Additionally, 56.93 percent of the students listen to radio for less than 15 minutes daily. 38.96 percent students watch TV/Cinema for one hour to two hours daily. 27.55 percent of the students surf the internet for one hour to two hours daily. It was apparent that most of the students like to watch realty shows than news. Sports news and entertainment news in the newspapers constituted the primary source of interest for the students. 'Mass Media' was reported as the main source of information on both *Climate Change* (56.17 percent) and *Global Warming* (49.01 percent) by the students, whereas, 'New media' like the internet and 'Interpersonal Communication' sources were reported as the main source by almost an equal (12.63 percent and 12.48 percent) number of respondents. Interestingly, 18.72 percent reported 'Do not know' when asked about their source of information on climate change.

Sinha *et al.* **(2014)** calculate that most of the respondents 132 (84.6%) access Internet on daily and regarding their preference of using social networking sites the majority of the respondent 121 (78%) preferred Face book followed by Linked-In 87 (56%) and Orkut 28 (18%).

Musa *et al.* **(2015)** find out the 111 of the respondents, only 28.8%of them was using social media, print media 1.8%, broadcast media 9.0 to report or share news while 60.4% never. This reveals that majority of the respondents was not using social media to share or report news.

Review of Literature

Yunus *et al.* (2015) calculate that most of the internet utilizing male SDAU students (47.86%) and majority of female SDAU students (60.00%) had 1 to 2 years experience of internet use. Majority of the internet utilizing male SDAU students (MPS 94.64) and female SDAU students (MPS 98.33) preferred hostel for internet use. The finding reveal that most of the internet utilizing male SDAU students (43.57%) and female SDAU students (36.67%) did not spent any money expenditure incurred to use internet. Majority of internet utilizing male SDAU students (66.42%) and (63.33%) female SDAU students had used internet facility every day.

Parvathamma and Shinde (2015) findings of the study reveal that majority of the students visit library daily or at least twice in a week and spend less than two hours during their visit. They visit library to borrow text books, general books in Horticulture and allied fields, read newspapers, magazines, and Indian and foreign journals. Reference sources such as dictionaries, encyclopedia are consulted rarely. Majority of the students never accessed bibliographic databases on CD/ROM or DVD and web resources.

Yebowaah (2017) calculate that use of electronic resources by lecturers of the University for Development Studies, Wa campus. The study recommended that efforts to improve the use of e-resources in the Library should include ways of creating user awareness, training/workshops for users and staff, and responding to the challenges confronting utilization.

Utpal (2017) calculate that majority of our sample students (43.8%) spend 1-5 hours in a week. Those who use facebook between 6-10 hours, 11-20 hours and 21-30 hours are 37.5%, 15.5% and 3.1% respectively. There is no single student who is live on facebook 24 hours. Equal number of male and female students spent time between 1-5 hours intervals and 6-10 hours intervals and their percentage are 43.8 and 37.5 respectively. No female students spent time more than 20 hours on facebook.

2.4 Relationship between independents variable with those of dependents

Variable:

Bandura (1994) calculate that they have the ability to enact a successful behavior and that it will be effective might be swayed through access to others, a mechanism often associated with social capital. Simply having access to a student-focused online community may have helped students believe that they would be able to reach other students who could provide help, even though use of the site is not directly related to expectations of academic success. Future work is needed to understand the relationship between these variables and how future interventions might capitalize on the endings ,we have outlined.

George, et al., (2006) calculate that the graduate students' information seeking behaviour was influenced by people, primarily academic staff, in addition to other students, friends, university library staff and people outside the university. Graduate students, who rely heavily on the internet, preferred online resources, which they found on the internet and the university library intranet. The findings of the study have implications for academic libraries in relation to the information behaviour of their students. Specifically, they affected university library instruction, availability of resources, and education of students and instructional leadership of academic staff.

Sheldon (2008) found that students use Facebook and other websites to pass time, be entertained, and maintain existing relationships with others. It seemed that college students were using social media sites to communicate with others as well as to occupy free time when they were bored.

West *et al.* (2009) calculate that making new friends over social media websites was not that important to college students. It appears that maintaining existing relationships with friends and family was a more important result of social media. "Lurking," or spending time looking at other users' profiles without having communication with them, was a significant reason for students to be on social networking sites.

Review of Literature

Baker and Oswald (2010) found that the individuals who used Facebook for communication had better quality friendships. Using social media sites helped improve the quality of relationships between users. Some reasons for improving quality of relationships through using Facebook included: it was easier to get to know others better without having face-to-face conversation, users felt more comfortable, and users spent more time communicating over the computer so they gained more social support.

Anie (2011) showed that lack of searching skills ranked first among inhibitors for both sexes (96.1% for males and 91.4% for females). This is because ICT is not fully implemented and embraced in tertiary institutions in Nigeria. Some students own laptops but use them to watch films or listen to music. Frequent interruption of electricity supply ranked second. The "Power Holding Company of Nigeria" (PHCN), which is responsible for generating and distributing electricity, has not been able to ensure a steady supply of power. This has also deprived the students from effective use of the digital library especially at night.

Imaita (2011) the study, the media, boys are getting obsessed with their body because they always see well-built men in magazines and television shows. Staying fit has never been an issue but there is an alarming increase in the number of people who adhere to obsessive weight training and use anabolic steroids and dietary supplements that promise these boys bugger muscles and more stamina for lifting. With regard to sex, three out of four teenagers say that the television shows and movies make it seem normal for children their age to engage in sexual relations. The young teens regard the entertainment media as the number one source of information about sexuality and sexual health. Being open about sex and how they talk to their girlfriends or boyfriends about it is largely because of what they see and hear.

Chokker *et al.* (2012) reports the findings of a survey administered to 268 secondary students studying in four English medium schools in Delhi, the capital city of India. With 54 percent males and 46 percent females, the sample consisted of students from middle and upper - middle class families studying in 12th standard. The questionnaire was devised by an international team and was designed to investigate students' willingness to undertake certain specific pro-environmental actions and their beliefs in the efficacy of these same actions in reducing global warming.

Maqableh (2015) found that the respondents demographic profile, it revealed that they are typically females and most of them in the second and third year level (sophomores and juniors), with ages between 20 - 23 years old. Results also show that they are using Facebook heavily given that 38.5% of students are spending three hours daily, and about 40% of them are spending more than 10 hours per week.

Kolawole *et al.* (2015) calculate that Facebook (751 or 90.2%) and Twitter (646 or 77.6%) were the most commonly accessible social media networks while meeting with friends (651 or 78.2%), getting news (566 or 67.9%), communication (554 or 66.5%) and online learning (450 or 54.0%) were major purposes for social media usage among the undergraduate students. Low level of social media addiction and positive self-perception were also established among the undergraduate students. Self perception is significantly positively related with social media utilization social ($r = .181$, $p<0.01$) and social media addiction ($r = .195$, $p<0.01$). The relative contribution of social media utilization and social media addiction to self perception were ($\beta = .111$, $t = 2.852$) and ($\beta = .140$, $t = 3.569$) respectively.

Kiragu (2015) on the negative influence of social media on our communities asserted that, the increasing access to smart devices by young teenagers has enhanced their capacity to access sexual materials from the internet and share it with their peers through the widely available social network channels. He further, highlights that the privacy accorded by these social media accounts contributes to their popularity among teenagers as avenues of sharing explicit content. This, study however, did not establish the association between the social media usage and sexual behavioral practices on secondary students specifically.

Goel and Singh (2016) calculate that results indicate that privacy concerns ($r = -.387$, $p<.01$) exhibit negative and significant relationship with beliefs and attitudes of management students toward social media use in education. However, perceived ease of use (r= .557, p<.01) is found to be positively correlated to beliefs and attitudes of management students toward social media use in education.It can thus be established that if the students have high privacy related concerns while using social media, their attitude is negatively affected and in case they perceive social media to be easy to use, their attitude towards social media is positively affected.

Manjunath and Babu (2018) calculate that majority of the respondents (36.2%) replied that they are purpose of seeking information for writing papers followed by for updating knowledge (25.4%), for preparing for competitive exams (23.8%), for writing assignments (7.7%), for preparing examinations (4.6%) and remain of them (2.3%) replied that they are purpose of seeking information for entertainment.

2.5 Constraints in utilization of mass media by the students and suggestions to overcome the constraints:

Huesmann and Eron (1986) Suggested the acceleration rate of violent crime with the entrance of television in most children's homes; it is not surprising that television has become the scapegoat. Of all the mass media, television violence has the greatest potential for both short-term and long-term effects upon children.

Mishra *et al.* (2005) calculate that a majority of the students (85.7%) used the Internet. The findings of the study also showed that 61.5% of the males and 51.6% of the females used the Internet for preparing assignments. A majority of the respondents i.e. 83.1% male and 61.3% female respondents indicated that they faced the problem of slow functioning of Internet connections.

Canary and Lakey (2006) calculate that communication competence skills can be learned and honed through education and experience. Therefore, future interventions should consider attempts to increase communication competence skills through education and training in an attempt to reduce depression and other health outcomes, keeping in mind other variables (e.g., social support, job stress) that may have a mediating effect on these variables.

Kaur and Verma (2006) described the use of the electronic resources by the TIET library, Patiala. In this case study, a survey was conducted, using a questionnaire to collect the data. Questionnaire was administered to all the library users including students, research scholars and faculty members. The paper also examines the interest of the users abut internet, Info net, CD-Rom data bases and other services provided by the library. Finally, it highlights the suggestions given by the users for improvement of electronic resources.

Okello-Obura and Magara (2008) calculate that students used electronic resources to obtain academic information and current awareness, and the major constraints faced were the shortage of computers, unreliable internet connection, and lack of skills. The respondents mentioned that they derived a lot of benefits from electronic resources as they were able to gain access to a wider range of information and that access to quality information improved their academic performance.

Khongtim and Marbaniang (2008) suggested that the different sources of information used by them and it try to bring out the problems they face during the search attempt for information. They also tried to find out whether the students are using the library as one of the main sources of information or not. Findings show that most of the students will depend on the library for their study and there are still many more students that do not use internet as one of their sources of information. In fact, other sources such as journals, newspapers, television are also less reliable to the students.

Lenhart *et al.* (2010) examined college students that face-to-face communication competencies may likely influence social support network size and satisfaction, which, in turn, may influence depression. Given that 72% of young adults online in 18–29 years of a used social networking sites, such as facebook. The present study seeks to examine the role of face-to-face and computer-mediated communication (CMC) competencies and how they relate to social support network satisfaction and to depression.

Chauhan (2010) calculate that majority of the respondents their dine to used the internet daily or twice wook by their won. 82% of the farmer their children to make positive use of internet at time. Internet age and mass media exposure are significance and positively correlated with pinion of the farmers about the use of the internet for the forming community.

Ansari and Zuberi (2010) calculate that a large majority (78.5 percent) know about electronic resources. Lack of knowledge and networking problems are the main reasons for not using electronic resources. The Significant amount of academics (90%) believe electronic resources are reliable, however majority of the respondents consider only those electronic resources are reliable which are produced by authentic organization or publisher.

Sinha (2010) found that only 80 (24.7%) of the respondents were using the internet for all purposes followed by 56 (17.3%) who accessed the internet for research purpose, sending and receiving e-mails and making personal contacts by using social networking sites whereas 48 (14.8%), 44 (13.6%) and 40 (12.3%) are surfing the internet for e-mails, updating knowledge and preparing class notes/lecture respectively. The study suggested that more terminals had to be added for accessing internet and uninterrupted power supply and more number of social sciences, humanities and languages journals have to be added.

Mostofa and Mamun (2011) found a high percentage of internet use among students. More than 56 percent of the respondents use the internet for educational purposes. The access point for them is mostly the university. Google and Yahoo! search engines are found to be more widely used than other search engines. The major problem faced by the students in their use of the internet includes slow access speed. It is further recommended that the bandwidth should be increased to overcome the problem of slow connectivity of the university to internet and more computers with the latest specifications and multimedia facilities should be provided.

Cox *et al.* (2011) calculate that the receive email (80.7%), send email (73.7%), search the internet (64.9%), send email attachments (57.9%), use black board Reg. (54.4%), and type a lab or project report (952.6%). Of 40 specific tasks, 19 were required in less than 10% of all courses. The least frequently required tasks included: program a database (0%), create an Excel Reg. Pivot table (1.8%), create a spreadsheet macro (1.8%), use file software (1.8%), and create a web page (3.5%).

Raghuram and Vatnal (2011) calculate that maximum number of faculty members (58.3%) learnt the UGC-INFONET programme through library orientation, and 43.75% (35) research scholars learnt from their teachers and research guide. The results also reveals that majority of the social science users (91.7% faculty members and 96.26% research scholars) are expecting more number of journals to be added in the UGC-INFONET programme.

Ahmad *et al.* (2012) shows that 46.31% of the Research Scholars indicated that Lack of system speed while accessing was the major problem followed by 44.21% of Research Scholars faced difficulty in accessing full-text, 32.63% of the Research Scholars indicated slow internet connectivity as well as lack of sufficient E-journals, 21.10% of Research Scholars responded that limited access terminals is the problem, and 16.84% responded that they face difficulty in finding the relevant information, 20% responded that they face retrieval problem, 15.79%, respondent indicated that they faced insufficient time and training. A few including loading (Retrieval Problem) followed by 13.68% indicate that poorly designed website make problem, followed by 5.26% responded they face problem to read the journal from the computer. Only 2.1% respondents face other type of problem.

Ahmed (2013) calculates that the students are not at all satisfied with the current level of university subscribed online resources. The students identified limited access to computers and slow download speed as major problems. These problems do affect electronic resources use by students in these universities. However, the problems are mainly related to poor ICT infrastructure which may also lead to other drawbacks such as unwillingness to use the resources regularly and thus low satisfaction with such resources.

Ajiboye *et al.* (2013) findings of the study also revealed that the use of the tools has impacted positively on the postgraduate students' social and academic life and also broaden their global knowledge of diverse issues. The major constraint to their use of the tools is that of Internet fluctuations. Records the highest percentage is that of Internet fluctuations which recorded a 70.5% response rate followed by financial constraints with a percentage of 52.4%.

Wright *et al.* (2013) calculated that although both face-to-face and Facebook support network satisfaction may be associated with reductions in self-reported depression scores, face-to-face support network satisfaction appears to have a larger effect on reducing depression than Facebook support network satisfaction. Yet, this finding may be tied to the specific population used in this study (college students).

Tariq and Zia (2014) showed that they used electronic resources for class assignments and to get updates about their specialty. The main barriers to access and use were slow network connection, power failure, viruses, and subscription issues. Furthermore, the users also need to get trained for an effective use of these resources.

Kumar *et al.* (2014) findings of the survey reveal useful facts about the Information Seeking Behaviour by Kurukshetra University Kurukshetra. 28.92% of the respondents were always use the information by the library daily, and same 28.92% sometimes with the requirement of information by the subject of interest. In fact 22.31% of the respondents were always uses the information weekly, 3.30% sometimes with the statement. Only 16.52% of the respondents were always uses the information twice in a week. On the basis of the findings, it was suggested that in order to improve the speed of Internet should be increased and the respondents can speedily access the information and utilize the information by the important work i.e. research work, education work, writing paper/presenting paper, administrative work, entertainment and also their download relevant materials. So provide better provision for the library should organized training programme for the information professionals so that they can know about different search interface, latest changes of the journals site and develop sophisticated searching and retrieval skills or techniques. Most of respondents were suggested that Kurukshetra University Kurukshetra should take necessary steps to utilize the library must take improve the internet, and aware the students about E-Journals & E-resources available in INFLIBNET.

Bankole *et al.* (2015) Calculate the respondents were requested to indicate the constraints faced in the use of electronic resources. The most common constraint in insufficient skill to retrieved needed information cited by 65 (38.2%) of respondents. Next was difficulty in finding relevant information mentioned by 56 (33.0%) respondents, lack of time to access electronic information resources (25.3%) and frequent power outage by 42(24.7%) respondents. The other constraints mentioned by over 20% of respondents were slow internet speed (22.4); information overload (21.8), limited access to an internet point (21.2 %).

Kumar (2015) analyzed the awareness and usage of EIRS among the Teachers and Students of IIMS. The study demonstrated and elaborated the various aspects of the purpose of using EIRS, types, methods and linking pattern of EIRS. The study discussed with the reason for using EIRS and suggested to make the EIRS more beneficial.

Viswanathan (2016) attempted to deal with user's opinion regarding the usage of Library Electronic Resources of selected arts and science colleges in Tamil Nadu. This paper provided few suggestions for the effective use of the resources among arts and science college libraries.

Krishna and Kumari (2016) found the impact of information communication technology on information seeking behaviours of users i.e. library membership, time spent on ISB activities, problems faced while seeking information, purposes of seeking information, information seeking habits relevant to academic work, sources most convenient for information seeking, opinion about necessity of training for using electronic (ICT) resources, opinion about direct influence of ICT on study, teaching, research and extension activities, use of ICT based digital resources compare to traditional print resources. The outcome and suggestions of the study would be beneficial to take appropriate measures to improve ISB with the aid of ICT.

Haque *et al.*(2016) shows that most of respondents (Mean 3.06 and rank 1) stated their method of seeking information by discussion of library catalogue and consulting the experts in the field of related disciplines (rank-2), librarians / library staff (rank-3).

Secondly most of the respondents seek information for current information, research and writing articles. Sixty four percent faculty members access more documents was references from periodicals and text books. All of the faculty members and research scholars read and write library materials in English and Bengali. Most of the respondents faced problems while them seeking information i.e. inadequate library resources and inadequate physical facilities etc.

Enanu and Natarajan (2016) calculate that the awareness of the services provided by the library, the purpose and type of information the students were seeking, the accessing of internet facility and use of catalogue card with the satisfaction of the services provided. They are not satisfied with the reading hall and reference service. They also suggested to have more e-resources and more photocopiers for the serving the student community. LIS professionals should take initiative to introduce e-discovery tools for better searching the e-resources together.

Ali Amour El-Maamiry (2017) examined possible factors and problems in their searching habits, information seeking, use and retrieval in satisfying their needs. Therefore, the study focused on information seeking behavior of students and barriers to utilizing online resources to execute academic tasks. Students of University of Dubai ultimately, due to cultural effects adopt different searching processes, use different phrases and mostly spend more time to search for information to satisfy their needs. It is assumed that poorinformation skills are preventing them from searching information effectively.

Bala (2018) shows that research articles, and e-books are extensively used open access resources for course and research work. Training and online tutorials can be helpful in overcoming the problems faced by researchers in using OARs.

Chapter-III
RESEARCH METHODOLOGY

The chapter deals with description of procedure followed for carrying out the investigation. It contains the tools and techniques employed for data collection, the sampling procedure adopted as well as the devices used for analysis of data are also explained. The present investigation "Study on Mass Media Utilization Pattern of the Post Graduate students of agriculture in State Agriculture Universities of Uttar Pradesh." was conducted during the year 2019-2020 description of the methods and procedures of investigation used during the entire course of study are presented under the following heads:

3.1. Local of the study.

3.2. Sampling designs and selection of the respondents.

3.3. Selection of variables and their empirical measurements.

3.4. Procedure of data collection.

3.5. Statistical methods use.

3.1 Locale of the study

3.1.1 Selection of the district.

The study was conducted in Uttar Pradesh, is most populous state, accounts for the largest population and number of mass media subscribers. Hence selected purposively for the study. The selection of the district Ayodhya, Kanpur, Meerut, and Banda will be done purposively as the agriculture universities are situated in these district of Uttar Pradesh. Since the investigator is studying in Acharya Narendera Deva University of Agriculture & Technology, Kumargunj, Ayodhya, So it will be collect the required information from Acharya Narendera Deva University of Agriculture & Technology, Kumarganj, Ayodhya, Chandera Shekhar Azad University of Agriculture & Technology, Kanpur, Sardar Vallabhbhai Patel University of Agriculture & Technology, Meerut and Banda

University of Agriculture & Technology, Banda, in India. College of Agriculture from each university (Ayodhya, Kanpur, Meerut, & Banda) will be taken for the study purposely.

The district Ayodhya, is situated at $26.50^0 N$ latitude and $81.4^0 E$ longitude. Its total geographical area is 2643 square kilometer. The density of population is 1054 per square kilometer.

Table- 3.1.1: Information about the district Ayodhya (Census 2011)

S. No.	Particulars	Figure
1.	Gram panchayats	729
2.	Nyan panchayats	129
3.	Villages	1270
4.	Bus stop	42
5.	Railway station	17
6.	Total population	2468371
a.	Male	1258455
b.	Female	1209916
c.	Male Scheduled Caste Population	281284
d.	Female Scheduled Caste Population	2737663
e.	Male Scheduled Tribes Caste Population	469
f.	Female Scheduled Tribes Caste Population	462
g.	Population density(per square kilometer)	1054
h.	Sex ratio	961
7.	Total literacy percentage	60.21%

a.	Male literacy percentage		80.21%
b.	Female literacy percentage		60.72%
c.	Scheduled Caste literacy percentage		57.40%
d.	Scheduled Tribes Caste literacy percentage		68.70%
8.	Length of canal		1225
9.	Government tube wells		851
10.	Personal tube wells and pump set		78106
11.	Veterinary hospital		35
12.	Artificial insemination centers		76
13.	Primary health centers (Gov.)		15
14.	Junior basic school		1226
15.	Senior basic school		283
16.	High school and intermediate college		65
17.	Degree college		06
18.	Universities		02
19.	Total geographical area (sq.km.)		2643 Sq.km.
a.	Irrigated area (in ha.)		240 ha.
b.	Un- irrigated area (in ha.)		181 ha.
c.	Total cultivated area		421 ha.

Source: District H.Q. Ayodhya.

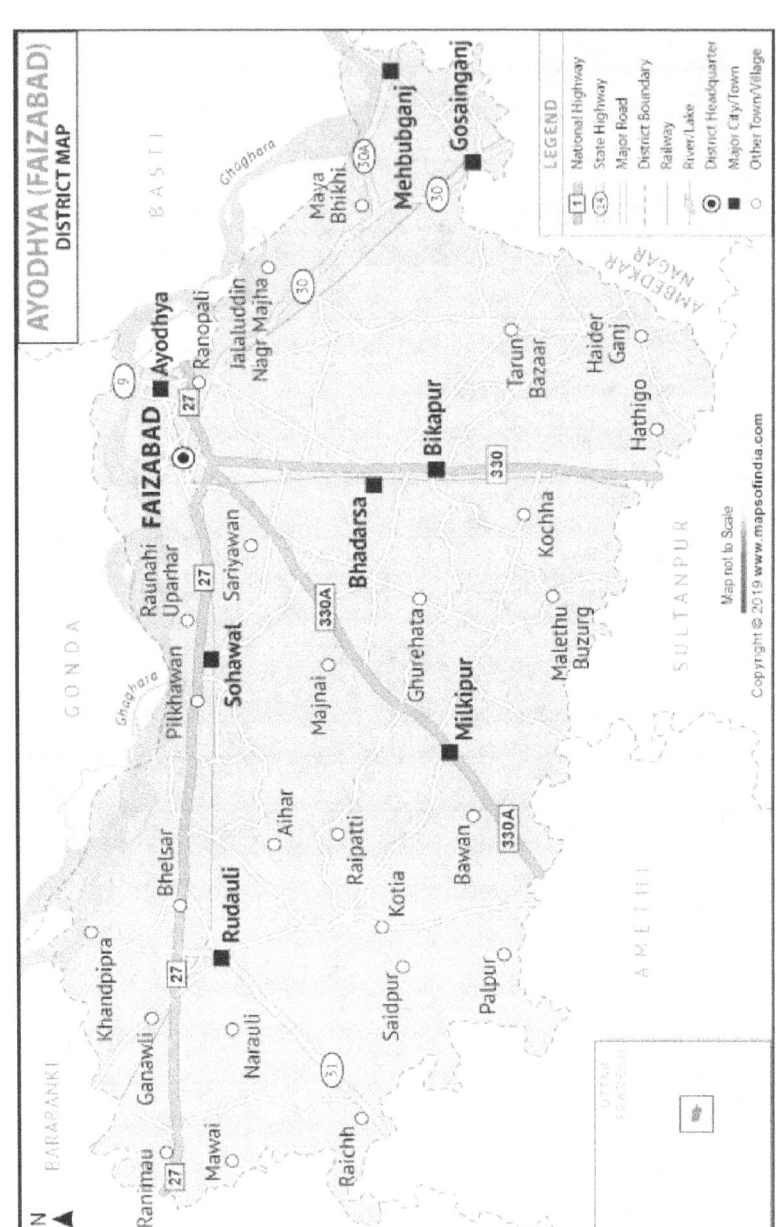

Fig.1 Map of Ayodhya District

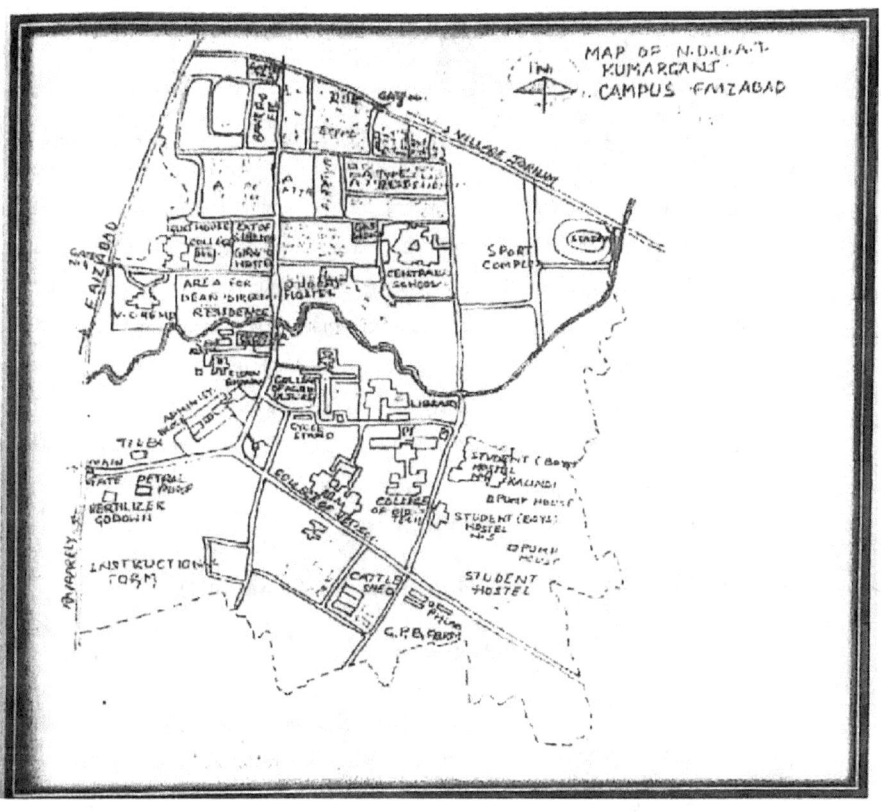

Fig.2 Map of Acharya Narendera Deva University of Agriculture & Technology, Kumarganj, (Ayodhya), U.P.

Research Methodology

The district Kanpur "Leather City of India" and "Manchester of the East", is situated at 26.50^0N latitude and 80.30^0E longitude. Its total geographical area is 403.70 square kilometer and the density of population is 6,900 per square kilometer. Kanpur Nagar Nigam area, 8 kilometers around KNN boundary with newly included 47 villages of Unnao district on the north-eastern side, it extends to Murtaza Nagar, in the west its limit is up to Akbarpur, Kanpur Dehat Nagar Panchayat limit, on the eastern side the limit has been expanded on the road leading to Fatehpur and in extended up to. The metropolitan region area includes the area of Shuklaganj Municipal Committee (Nagar Palika), Unnao Municipal Committee (Nagar Palika), Akbarpur Village Authority (Nagar Panchayat) and Bithoor Village Authority (Nagar Panchayat) area. In 1997–98, total metropolitan region area has increased to 89131.15 hectare out of which 4,743.9 hectare (5.31%) was non-defined (prohibited area) and rest 29,683 hectare and 54,704 hectare (61.39%) was urban and rural area respectively.

Table- 3.1.2: Information about the district Kanpur (Census 2011)

S. No.	Particulars	Figure
1.	Gram panchayats	645
2.	Nyan panchayats	114
3.	Villages	47
4.	Bus stop	35
5.	Railway station	8
6.	Total population	2,767,348
a.	Male	1,531,255
b.	Female	1236093
c.	Male Scheduled Caste Population	439603
d.	Female Scheduled Caste Population	377151
e.	Male Scheduled Tribes Caste Population	2108

Research Methodology

f.	Female Scheduled Tribes Caste Population		1645
g.	Population density(per square meter)		18,000/sq mi
h.	Sex ratio		855
7.	Total literacy percentage		84.37%
a.	Male literacy percentage		81.23%
b.	Female literacy percentage		63.54%
c.	Scheduled Caste literacy percentage		68.50%
e.	Scheduled Tribes Caste literacy percentage		63.40%
8.	Length of canal		1156
9.	Government tube wells		953
10.	Personal tube wells and pump set		84106
11.	Veterinary hospital		56
12.	Artificial insemination centers		87
13.	Primary health centers (Gov.)		25
14.	Junior basic school		1537
15.	Senior basic school		4621
16.	High school and intermediate college		86
17.	Degree college		18
18.	Universities		04
19.	Total geographical area (sq.km.)		403.70 km^2
a.	Irrigated area (in ha.)		214 ha.
b.	Un- irrigated area (in ha.)		146 ha.
c.	Total cultivated area		534 ha.

Source: District H.Q. Kanpur.

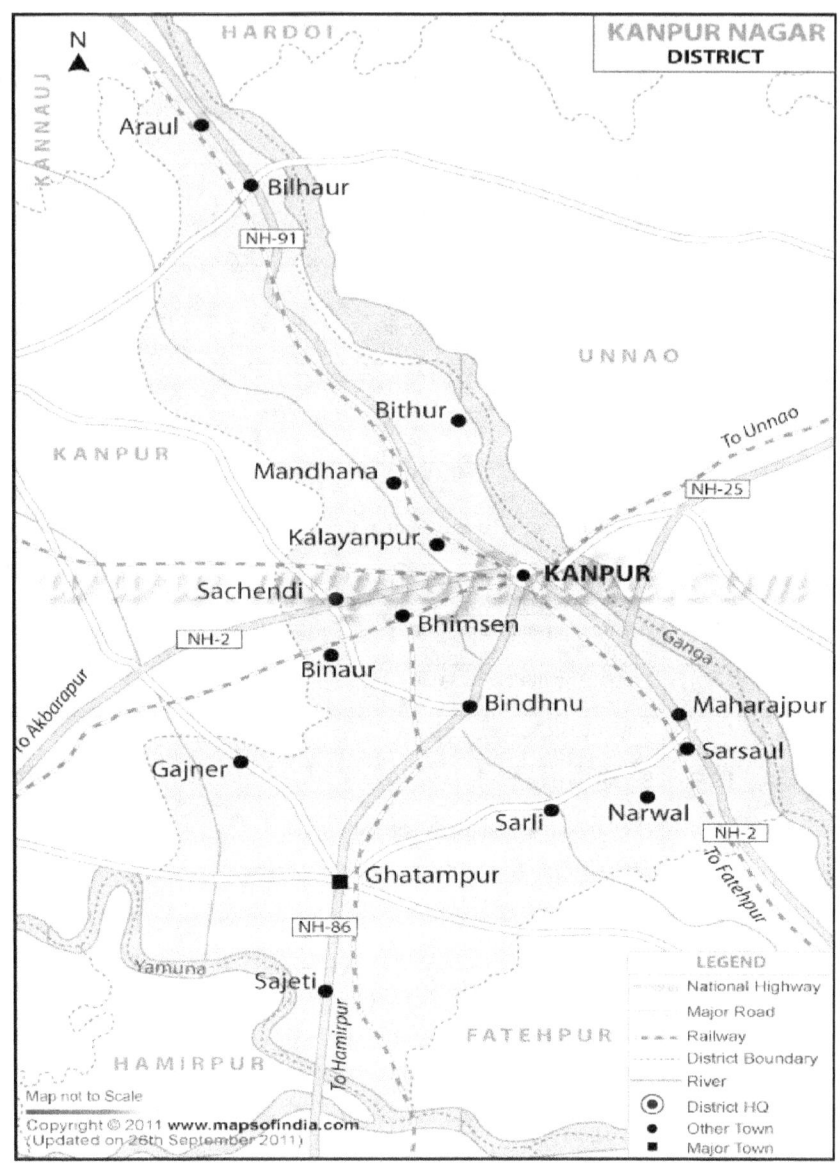

Fig. 3 Map of Kanpur district

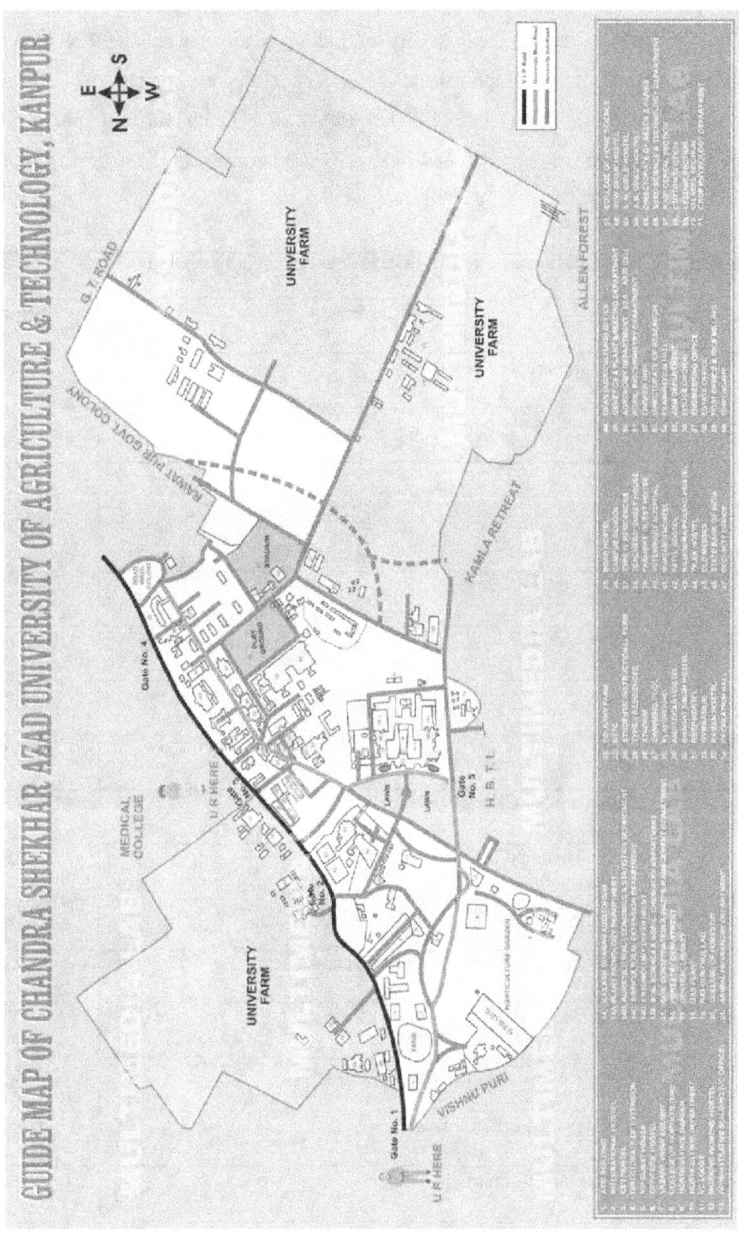

Fig. 4 Map of CSAUAT, Kanpur

Research Methodology

The district Meerut "Sports City of India", is situated at 28.99^0N latitude and 77.70^0E longitude. Its geographical area is 2,522 per square kilometer (974 sq mi). The municipal area (as of 2001) is 141.89 km^2 (54.78 sq mi) with the cantonment covering 35.68 km^2 (3,568.06 ha). The city lies 70 km (43 mi) northeast of the national capital New Delhi.

Table- 3.1.3: Information about the district Meerut (Census 2011)

S. No.	Particulars	Figure
1.	Gram panchayats	784
2.	Nyan panchayats	143
3.	Villages	1145
4.	Bus stop	45
5.	Railway station	5
6.	Total population	1,420,902
a.	Male	752,893
b.	Female	668,009
c.	Male Scheduled Caste Population	334198
d.	Female Scheduled Caste Population	289591
e.	Male Scheduled Tribes Caste Population	1828
f.	Female Scheduled Tribes Caste Population	1562
g.	Population density(per square kilometer)	8,300/km^2
h.	Sex ratio	887
7.	Total literacy percentage	76.28 %
a.	Male literacy percentage	81.57 %

b.	Female literacy percentage	70.36 %
c.	Scheduled Caste literacy percentage	71.70%
d.	Scheduled Tribes Caste literacy percentage	61.30%
8.	Length of canal	1432
9.	Government tube wells	659
10.	Personal tube wells and pump set	98593
11.	Veterinary hospital	67
12.	Artificial insemination centers	85
13.	Primary health centers (Gov.)	35
14.	Junior basic school	1351
15.	Senior basic school	385
16.	High school and intermediate college	69
17.	Degree college	285
18.	Universities	05
19.	Total geographical area (sq.km.)	2,522 km^2
a.	Irrigated area (in ha.)	353ha.
b.	Un- irrigated area (in ha.)	124ha.
c.	Total cultivated area	735 ha.

Source: District H.Q. Meerut.

Meerut District Map

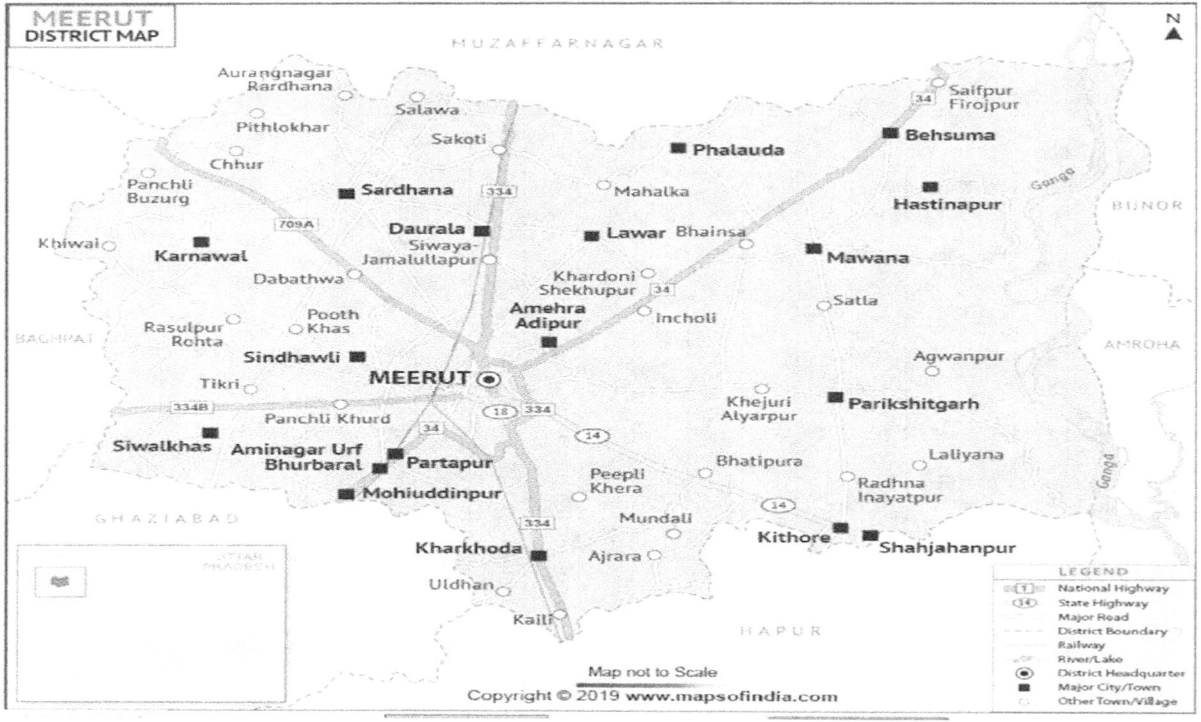

Fig. 5 Map of Meerut district

Research Methodology

The district Banda is situated at $25.483°N$ latitude and $80.333°E$ longitude. Its geographical area is 443.1 per square kilometer. This is the easternmost district of Bundelkhand. The division of the district into two has been done by splitting Banda district, tahsil and block-wise. Karwi and Mau Tahsils lying in the eastern and South-eastern direction comprising the Manikpur, Mau, Pahadi, Chitrakut and Ramnagar blocks from the present Chitrakut district. Banda, which forms one of the districts included under the general name of Bundelkhand, has formed an arena of contention for the successive races who have struggled for the sovereignty of India.

Table- 3.1.4: Information about the district Banda (Census 2011)

S. No.	Particulars	Figure
1.	Gram panchayats	356
2.	Nyan panchayats	154
3.	Villages	1536
4.	Bus stop	28
5.	Railway station	15
6.	Total population	154,428
a.	Male	82,116
b.	Female	72,312
c.	Male Scheduled Caste Population	208,184
d.	Female Scheduled Caste Population	179,671
e.	Male Scheduled Tribes Caste Population	82
f.	Female Scheduled Tribes Caste Population	81
g.	Population density(per square kilometer)	$350/km^2$

Research Methodology

h.	Sex ratio	881
7.	Total literacy percentage	82.05%
a.	Male literacy percentage	66.2%
b.	Female literacy percentage	53%
c.	Scheduled Caste literacy percentage	57.30%
d.	Scheduled Tribes Caste literacy percentage	41.90%
8.	Length of canal	157
9.	Government tube wells	261
10.	Personal tube wells and pump set	67
11.	Veterinary hospital	52
12.	Artificial insemination centers	47
13.	Primary health centers (Gov.)	1275
14.	Junior basic school	362
15.	Senior basic school	58
16.	High school and intermediate college	05
17.	Degree college	01
18.	Universities	15
19.	Total geographical area (sq.km.)	251 ha.
a.	Irrigated area (in ha.)	436 ha.
b.	Un- irrigated area (in ha.)	639 ha.
c.	Total cultivated area	

Source: District H.Q. Banda.

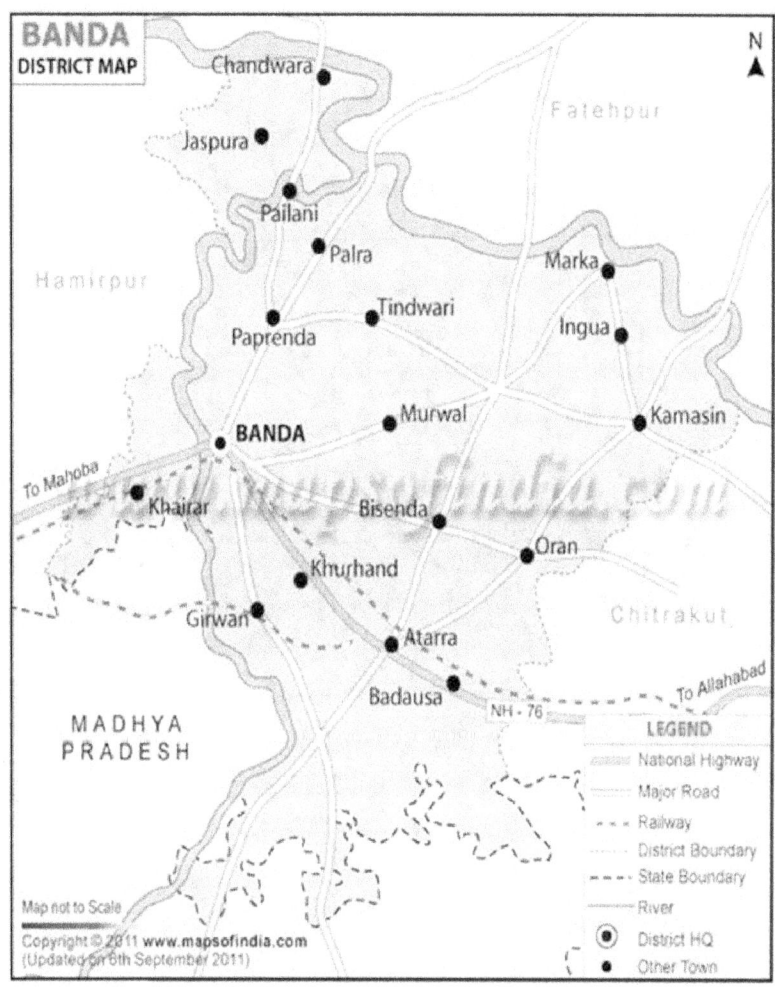

Fig. 6 Map of Banda district

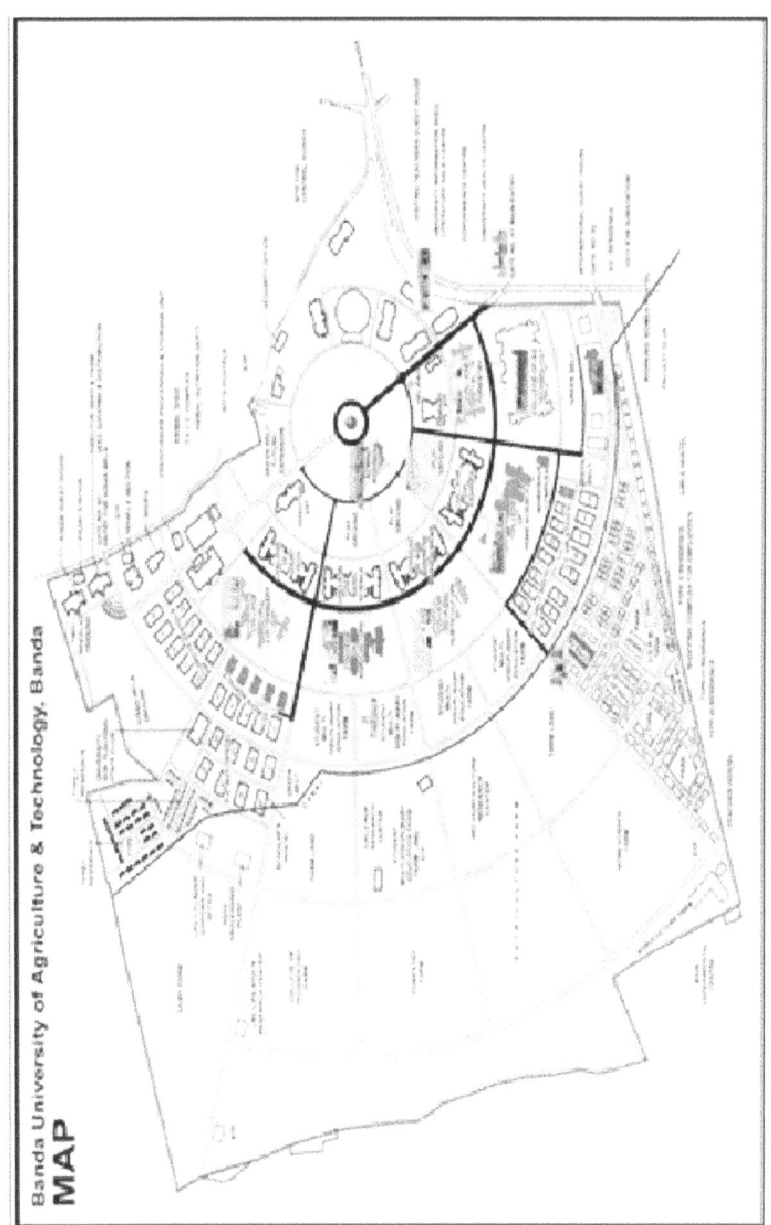

Fig. 7 Banda University of Agriculture and Technology, Banda

3.2.1: Sampling designs and selection of the respondents:

The Personal Interview schedule was prepared to see the study on mass media utilization pattern and knowledge extent among the Post Graduate students of agriculture in State Agriculture Universities of Uttar Pradesh. Selection of the respondents purposively was done by simple random sampling method from every agriculture college for each agricultural university in Uttar Pradesh. A its of all the students studying in P.G. classes in all four agricultural universities were prepared and out of that 30% of the students were selected as sample for study purpose. The total sample size 657 respondents, about the 30% total post graduate students sample size 197respondents were selected randomly all four universities college. Then, the Ex post-facto design is used to see the knowledge extent of mass media utilization pattern uses of Post Graduate students of agriculture. A schedule were be develop keeping objective the study in view and along with necessary scale developed by extension scientist were used to collect the primary data from the respondents. Respondents were contacted personally for data collection. The appropriate statistical tools and techniques were being applied to analyze the data and to draw inferences accordingly.

Table 3.2.1: Information about Universities situated in this district.

S. No.	Name of University	District
1.	(a) Dr. Ram Manohar Lohia Avadh University. (b) Acharya Narendera Deva University of Agriculture & Technology, Kumargunj,	Ayodhya, U.P.
2.	(a) Chhatrapati Shahu Ji Maharaj University, kalyanpur, (b) Chandera Shekhar Azad University of Agriculture& Technology, (c) Harcourt Butler Technical University (d) Rama University, Mandhana,	Kanpur, U.P.
3.	(a) Chaudhary Charan Singh University (b) Sardar vallabhbhai Patel University of Agriculture & technology	Meerut, U.P.

Research Methodology

	(c) Swami Vivekanand Subharti University	
	(d) Shobhit university	
	(e) IIMT University	
4.	(a) Banda University of Agriculture &Technology	Banda, U.P.

Table- 3.2.2: Information about selected District and Agriculture Universities:

S.N.	District	Total No. of Universities	Selected University	Design
1.	Ayodhya	2	Acharya Narendra Deva University of Agriculture &Technology, Nrendra Nagar, Ayodhya.(U.P.)	Purposively
2.	Kanpur	4	Chandra Shekhar Azad University of Agriculture &Technology, Kanpur.(U.P.)	Purposively
3.	Meerut	5	Sardar Vallabhbhai Patel University of Agriculture & Technology, Modipurum, Meerut. (U.P.)	Purposively
4.	Banda	1	Banda University of Agriculture & Technology, Banda. (U.P.)	Purposively

Table- 3.2.3: General information of the selected students, college with department:

S.N.	Universities	Total No. of department	Total No. college	Selected college	Total selected students	Total selected students about 30%
1.	A. N.D. U.A & T, Kumargunj, Ayodhya.	15	7	College of Agriculture	252	76

2.	C.S.A.U.A & T, Kanpur.	12	8	College of Agriculture	205	61
3.	S.V.P.U.A & T, Modipuram, Meerut	9	6	College of Agriculture	136	41
4.	B.U.A & T, Banda	7	4	College of Agriculture	64	19

3.3 Selection of variable and their empirical measurements

Table-3.3.1 Variable and their measurements.

Sr. No.	Variables	Empirical measurement
(A)	**Independent Variable**	
1	Age	Chronological age class developed and use
2	Caste	According to Indian constitution and use
3	Marital status	Scale developed and used
4	Land holding	Government of India category(1991)
5	Family type	Scale developed by Trivedi and pareek (1964) with minor modification
6	Family size	Scale developed by Trivedi and pareek (1964) with minor modification
7	Material possession	Schedule will be developed & used
8	Social participation	Saradha (2001)
9	Annual family income	Schedule will be developed & used
10	Housing pattern	Scale developed by Trivedi and pareek (1964) with minor modification

11	Extension contact	Index to be developed and used
12	Scientific orientation	Scale developed by Supe (1969) used with suitable modifications.
(B)	**Dependent Variables**	
1.	Knowledge extent	Schedule will be developed & used
2.	Utilization pattern of mass media	Schedule will be developed & used
C.	Constraints analysis	Perceived constraint from the students
D.	Suggestion to overcome the Constraints	Perceived suggestion from the students

A. **Independent variables:**

1.1- Age of respondents:

The age of the respondents as informed by them during personal interview was recorded. The age categories were, made according to mean and standard deviation duly computed for the purpose.

2.1 Caste:

Castes of the respondents were categorized into three categories as per government norms *viz.*

S. No.	Categories	Scores
(a)	General Caste (GEN)	1
(b)	Other Backward Caste (OBC)	2
(c)	Scheduled Cast (SC)	3
(d)	Scheduled tribes (ST)	4
(e)	Minority	5

a. General caste:

This category is concerned with Kshatriya, Brahmin, Vaishya and Kayastha etc.

b. Other Backward Caste:

It includes, Yadav, Gujjar, Chaurasia, Maurya, Kurmi, Kahar, Lohar, Barber etc.

c. Scheduled Caste:

This category is concerned with Kori, Chamar, Pasi, Washerman etc. for the study undertaken.

d. Schedule Tribes:

This category is concerned with Meena, Bahalia, etc.

e. Minority: Muslims, Christians, Sikhs, Buddhist, Janis, etc.

This category is concerned with

The scores were assigned to various caste categories as minority (5), schedule tribes (4) scheduled caste (3), backward caste (2) and general caste (1).

3.1 Marital status:

The score were assigned to two marital categories namely married The scale is self-developed and used the scoring was done as per the scale.

S. No.	Categories	Scores
(a)	Unmarried	0
(b)	Married	1

Research Methodology

4.1 Land holding:

The actual land holding in hectares were recorded as reported by the respondents a category made accordingly.

5.1 Family type:

Respondents were classified into following two groups on the basis of family types possessed by them. The scale developed by Supe (1969) with suitable modification was used and the scoring was done as per the scale. Respondents were grouped into two categories as per their family type.

S. No.	Categories	Scores
(a)	Nuclear/ Single family	1
(b)	Joint family	2

6.1 Family size:

Respondents were classified into following three groups on the basis of family size as under. The scale developed by Supe (1969) was used and the scoring was done as per the scale. Respondents were grouped into three categories as per their family size.

S. No.	Categories	Scores
(a)	Small family – up to 5 members	1
(b)	Medium family- (6-8) members	2
(c)	Large family- 9 and above members	3

7.1 Material possession at home:

(A) House holds materials possession:-

The scores assigned to various household materials with their scores in parenthesis were viz., gas cylinder/stove, pressure cooker, electric press, wall, clock, sewing machine, fan/cooler, smokeless stove, solar light, heater, induction cooker, double bed, sofa set, dining table, dressing table, chairs, cots, electric ketali, air-conditioner respectively.

(B) Communication media possession:-

The scores were assigned to various sources of communication with their scores in parenthesis were viz., T.V., radio, news-paper, internet, (1), agriculture journal, agriculture magazines, general magazines, agriculture books (2), V.C.R., D.V.D./V.C.D. player, laptop, desktop, tablet, D.T.H., tape recorder (3), and mobile, telephone, (4) respectively.

(C) Farm power:

The farm power materials included under study with their scores in parenthesis were (1) Tractor, (2) Power tiller, (3) Diesel engine, (4) Electric motor (5) Tub-well (6) Solar energy pump and (7) Electronic grinder respectively.

(D) Agriculture Implements:

It refers to the agricultural implements owned by the respondents. Scoring was given by self-developed index by investigator. The scores assigned to various farm materials with the respondents were Desi plough, cultivator, disc plough, seed drill, Rotavator, Cane Cutter Planter, chaff cutter, Combine harvester, Thresher, cane crusher, leveler (pata), sprayer duster, kudal, shovel, khurpi, sickle, and pata respectively.

8.1 Social participation:

For social participation of the respondents, the various categories viz., member of one organization, member of two organizations, and member of more than two organizations or office bearer was framed.

S. No.	Social participation	Scores
(a)	No participation	0
(b)	Participation in one organization	1
(c)	Participation in two organization	2
(d)	Participation in more than two organizations	3

9.1 Annual family income:

Annual family income of the respondents was calculated in money value with unit of rupees considering all the sources and grouped into three categories

The scale developed by Supe (1969) with suitable modification. Categories were mode as (1) mean + SD. (2) mean – S.D. and (3) mean $\pm$ S.D.

10.1 Housing pattern:

It refers to the habitation the students get constructed and live there with their family members. It is various types.

To find out the housing pattern of the respondents, four types of houses were categorized:

S. No.	Categories of Housing pattern	Scores
(a)	Pucca	1
(b)	Mixed	2
(c)	Kaccha	3
(d)	Hut	4

11.1 Extension contact with information sources:

It referred to the awareness of respondents about various extension activities and their extent of participation in them. To study the Information & Knowledge Receiving Sources with Mass Contact (IKRSMC) for measuring the contact with extension personnel scale was developed. So far as the contact of the respondents with each information sources is concerned, each source was measured on 7 point continuum (No contact, half yearly, quarterly, monthly, fortnightly, weekly and daily) and 0, 1, 2, 3, 4, 5 and 6 scores were assigned to them respectively. A rank order was placed to them for interpretation.

11. (A) General knowledge about mobile mass media pattern:

The General knowledge about mobile mass media pattern by the respondents the degree of actual knowledge to the responds at a time of investigation of available pattern of mobile mass media which one they use were dichotomized having yes/no, if the yes the respondents have assigned 1 score and if answer no, the respondents assign 0score.

The study was carried on use of mobile mass media by the respondents for general knowledge of mass media utilization pattern.

The general knowledge about mobile mass media pattern about the Function of mobile mass media pattern, Recharge top up senses, Recharge provider company, Mobile mass media pattern provider company, Which is used network about mobile mass media pattern and Who is used of mobile mass media pattern. The range of score obtained by the respondents mighty very in low medium and high range in the mass media user's test which indicated the development level of the respondents it was shows by percentage respectively.

12.1 Scientific orientation:

The scale developed by Supe (1969) was used to measure the scientific orientation consisting of ten statements with some modification, which were all positive. The scale was administered on five points scale *viz.*, strongly agree, agree, undecided, disagree and strongly disagree. The scores were assigned as 5, 4, 3, 2, and 1, respectively for all the statements. The respondents were categorized into three categories such as low, medium and high. On the basis of total scores obtained such as low, medium and high. On the basis of total scores obtained the respondents following procedure of (i) mean- S.D. (Low), (ii) Mean ± S.D. (Medium) and (iii) Mean + S.D. (High).

B. Dependent variable:

1.1 Knowledge extent of the students about using the mass media pattern:

The purpose of the study, knowledge was defined as the awareness, extent and manner of the use of the mass media utilization pattern than measured by knowledge test used in this study. Knowledge extent about the uses of mass media utilization pattern by the respondents. Knowledge test developed by the investigator and used. The modifications in the existing knowledge test were in relation to item namely uses, function, services and advantage. All the question for knowledge were dichotomized having two dimension yes/no, if the answer was yes the respondents were assigned 1 score in and if answer no, the respondents were assigned 0 score.

The study was carried on knowledge extent of the mass media utilization pattern by the PG agriculture students.

The range of scores obtained by the respondents might vary in low, medium and high range in the knowledge test which indicated the knowledge extent of the respondents. It was categorized into three categories *viz*. (I) Mean-S.D. (II) Mean ± S.D. (III) Mean ± S.D. respectively.

1. **(A) Have you know of mass media pattern?**

    For the purpose of study, the respondents answer the know of mass media utilization pattern about knowledge extent to the respondents degree of actual known to the respondents to the score is (1) and if not have knowledge the score is (0).

1. **(B) Do you have knowledge about the following function of mass media pattern?**

Research Methodology

For the purpose of study, the respondents give the answer the function of mass media utilization pattern about knowledge extent to the respondents degree of actual known to the respondents to the score is (1) and if not have knowledge the score is (0).

1. **(C) Do you know about the following services of mass media pattern?**

    The respondents answer about the mass media utilization pattern to knowledge extent by the respondents the degree of actual known to the respondents about usage mass media if they had information the score is (1) and if not have information the score is (0).

1. **(D) Do you know about the agency/Institutes which, provides need information related to agriculture development and its allied viz. Dairy, Fisheries, Agro-forestry, Horticulture, Agricultural Extension etc. through mass media pattern?**

    The purpose of the study, usage of mass media utilization pattern was refers to the knowledge extent about the agriculture and it is allied sector viz. dairy, fisheries, agro-forestry, horticulture, agriculture extension etc. development. All the question for the respondents was dichotomized having two dimension yes/ no, if the answer yes the assigned 1 score and if answer no, the respondents have assigned 0 score.

1. **(E) Do you know about following specific information needed about your better future through mass media pattern?**

    The study was conducted to knowledge extent of the respondent for future development through mass media utilization pattern and the all question related to respondents for better future. The question for students was dichotomized having two dimension yes/no, if the answer yes the assigned 1 score and if answer No the respondents have assigned 0 score.

1. **(F) Which, services known by the student's group via mass media pattern?**

For the purpose of study, usage of the mass media utilization of pattern to known knowledge extent in provider of mass media services. The respondents the degree of actual known tote respondents was dichotomized having two dimension yes/ no, if the answer yes the assigned 1 score and if answer no, the respondents have assigned 0 score.

1. **(G) What benefits/advantages do you know from using mass media pattern in communicating information?**

    For the purpose of study, the respondents give the answer the benefits/ advantage of mass media utilization pattern about knowledge extent to the respondents degree of actual known to the respondents to the score is (1) and if not have knowledge the score is (0).

1.2 Knowledge extent of the students about educational atmosphere in your university related mass media pattern:

The study was conducted to knowledge extent of the respondent about educational atmosphere in the university through mass media utilization pattern and the all question related to respondents for known educational atmosphere. The question for students was dichotomized having two dimension yes/no, if the answer yes the assigned 1 score and if answer No the respondents have assigned 0 score.

1.3 Knowledge extent of the students about contact with information sources in your university:

It referred to the knowledge extent of respondents about various contact with information sources in his university and their extent of participation in them. So far as the contact of the respondents with each information sources in his university is concerned, each source was measured on 7 point continuum (No contact, half yearly, quarterly, monthly, fortnightly, weekly and daily) and 0, 1, 2, 3, 4, 5 and 6 scores were assigned to them respectively. A rank order was placed to them for interpretation.

(A) Used of different type mass media by the students for his development:

It referred to the awareness of the respondents and usage of different type mass media utilization pattern to his development by the respondents. All question in the mass media utilization pattern used and which one best for the respondents were respondent assigned a score of very useful, less useful, not useful if the answer was very useful the respondents assigned a score of (1) if the answer was less useful the respondents assigned a score of (2) if the answer was not useful the respondents a score of (0) in respectively.

2.1 Utilization pattern of mass media for the collection of information to different purpose:

It was operational as the degree to which the respondents oriented towards mass media utilization pattern for information receiving and transfer of technology, entertainment, data collection and transfer, and medium of Preparation, Reading, Agriculture practices managements, development of Knowledge, skill and attitude development, etc. All question of the mass media utilization pattern used were dichotomized having correct and incorrect if the answer was correct the respondents was assigned a score of (1) and if the answer was incorrect the respondents was assigned a score (0)

Constraints analysis:

The response of respondents was indicated the degree of seriousness of constraints as faced by deferent mass media pattern utilization. The frequency distribution was done and percentage was calculate for description. The Perceived constraint from the students side a list of all possible problems under categories viz. related to slow network, money problem, Wi-Fi not available in the university campus, light problem, internet facility not available, lack of time to using mass media utilization pattern for gathering information, language problem when using mass media utilization pattern, heavy class work load in study than not have time to use of mass media pattern, new mobile phone/ new mass media material is very costly to not purchasing by the respondents and improper and costaly distribution of mass material viz. newspapers, magazines, posters, Demonstration, exhibition, film show, agriculture books, etc. The seriousness of every constraint was measured to find out the facts. The respondents there after tabulated on the basis of frequency of the respondents and ranked order was given to each constraint respectively.

Suggestion to measures:

Suggestion to overcome the constraints relating to mass media utilization pattern by post graduate students in agriculture. The frequency distribution was done and percentage was calculated for description. The Perceived suggestion from the students side a list of all possible suggestion under categories viz. related to improving networking system, proper provide scholarship and decreasing university fee with help of any other Govt. economic help, Wi-Fi proper available in all university campus, proper light facility provide 24hur with help of inviter, internet facility provide in each hostel , students some time to using mass media utilization pattern for gathering information, language problem reduce with help of expert when using mass media utilization pattern, heavy class work load is decreasing in study. Proper time to use of mass media pattern, new mobile phone/ new mass media material is low cost to purchasing by the students and proper and reducing of cost distribution of mass material viz. newspapers, magazines, posters, Demonstration, exhibition, film show, agriculture books, etc.

Procedure of data collection:

A structure will be developed in schedule for data collection was designed and exercised by interviewing with few respondents for pre-testing. Selection of the respondents will be done by simple random sampling method from every agriculture college for each agricultural university in Uttar Pradesh. A list of all the students studying in P.G. classes in all four agricultural universities will be prepared and out of that 30% of the students will be selected as sample for study purpose. Then, the suitable modification was made according toned of this study. Thereafter, that data were collected from the respondents through personal interview technique.

Statistical methods used:

The 'percentage' and 'average' S.D. and correlation was used for making simple interpretation.

(I) Percentage (%):

The frequency of a particular cell was divided by the total number of respondents or (MPS) in that particular category and multiplied by 200 for calculating the percentage.

(II) Average ($\overline{X}$):

The average ($\overline{X}$) was calculated by adding the total scores obtained by the respondents and divided it by the total number of respondents using the following formula:

$$(\overline{X}) = \frac{\sum X}{N}$$

Where,

($\overline{X}$) = Average or mean

$\sum x$ = Total number of scores obtained by respondents

N = Total number of respondents

(III) Standard deviation:

Standard deviation is the square root of mean of the squares of all deviations, the directions being measured from the arithmetic mean of the distribution. It was commonly developed by symbol sigma (σ).

$$S.D. (\sigma) = \sqrt{\frac{\sum d^2}{n}}$$

Where,

σ = Standard deviation

d = Deviation of variables mean

n   =   Total number items

(IV) Correlation coefficient (r):

The coefficient of simple correlation (r) in a measure of the mutual relationship between two variables that in *i.e.* x and y, where relationship is measured and commonly termed as product movement correlation coefficient and is computed by the following formula:

$$r = \frac{\sum (X-\bar{X})(Y-\bar{Y})}{\sqrt{\sum (X-\bar{X})^2 \cdot \sum (Y-\bar{Y})^2}}$$

Where,

r = correlation coefficient

X = value of x independents variables

$\bar{X}$ = mean of X independents variable

Y = value of Y dependents variables

$\bar{Y}$ = mean of Y dependents variable

Chapter-IV

CONCEPTUAL FRAME WORK

This chapter deals with the conceptual frame work of variables related to study under taken. It is furnished as below:

(1) **Adoption:** It is mental process through which an individual passes from first hearing about a new idea (innovation) to its final use.

(2) **Age:** It refers to the chronological age of the respondent in number of years completed by him at the time of interview.

(3) **Annual income:** It refers to total income in rupees earned by the respondent from all sources in a particular year.

(4) **Bibliography:** List of books or other written materials placed for reference after a piece of academic writing or appearing as a separate publication.

(5) **Block :** A block is a unit of planning and development. This is an administrative means for taking the problems of rural people in their entirely in a concerted and co-coordinated manner.

(6) **Caste:** Caste is a permanent type of social stratification of the society into higher and lower categories.

(7) **Category:** A class, group or type based on some traits.

(8) **Communication media possession:** These are the means by which information or knowledge is passed on from one group or individual to another.

(9) **Constraints:** Problems or hurdles faced by the respondents in adoption of potato production technology.

(10) **Correlation:** A statistical measure showing the extent to which two variables are related not necessarily in a causal relationship; the magnitude of a correlation can vary from -1.00 to + 1.00.

(11) Data: Data are defined as facts, figures either known or available information.

(12) Economic motivation: It means that the individual is oriented towards achievement of maximum economic gain such as maximization of farm profits.

(13) Education: It refers to the level of formal education obtained by the respondents.

(14) Family size: It refers to the number of persons living in a family.

(15) Family types: It is of two types viz., single family and joint family. In a single family system, the father, mother and their children are considered while in a joint family system, the members of two and three generations along with relatives and servants live together under one roof with common fooding system.

(16) Family: All members of house hold who live together under one roof and one man guidance. They eat together and share their responsibilities in the interest of their family members.

(17) Household: a group of person normally living together and taking food from common kitchen

(18) Housing pattern: It refers to the habitation; the villagers get constructed and live there in with their family members. It is of various types *viz.*, Hut, Kuchcha, Mixed and Puckka.

(19) Illiteracy: It refers to the inability of a persons to read and write

(20) Illiterate: The term illiterate is used to designate a person who can not read and write, and has/had no formal schooling or its equivalent.

(21) Information: information is difference in matter energy that effect's uncertainty in a situation where a choice exits among a set of alternatives. So, information is something which reduces uncertainty.

(22) Interview: interviews are conducted with selected individuals/respondents. On decided topic which quickly reveal a wide range of opinion, attitude and strategies and finding

(23) **Knowledge:** Knowledge is the degree of awareness of a particular subject or field as a study. In this context, it is confined to the knowledge of potato grower about different package of practices undertaken by them.

(24) **Material possession:** Operationally defined as the general materials possessed by the respondents including recreational, farm implements, machines domestic materials, communication and transports.

(25) **Mean ($\overline{X}$):** A measure of central tendency, the sum of all observations/ items divided by their numbers, more popularly known as arithmetic mean. It is indicated by sign ($\overline{X}$).

(26) **Motivation:** The process of initiating conscious and purposeful action.

(27) **Objectives:** Objectives are expressions of the ends towards which our efforts are directed.

(28) **Occupation:** The main occupation is that which generates income more than 50 % while the subsidiary below than that.

(29) **Probability:** An estimate of the chance or livelihood that a particular thing or event will occur.

(30) **Purposive sample:** A type of non probability sample in which the elements to be included in the sample are selected by the researcher on the basis of special characteristics or typicality's of the respondents.

(31) **Random sampling:** The process in which all units of population have an equal chance of being selected for investigation.

(32) **Range:** A measure of dispersion; a difference score obtained by subtracting the smallest score from the largest score in the distribution.

(33) **Reference:** Note in a publication referring the reader to another passage source person who supplies a recommendation for some one seeking employment or an introduction.

(34) Respondents: The person who responds the questions asked by the investigator in a survey with the help of interview schedule. They are the people from whom, the social researchers usually obtain data required for their research work.

(35) Risk orientation: It refers to degree to which the respondents is oriented towards the risk uncertainty and has courage to face the problems.

(36) Sample: Some selected units from the universe of the population who represent the universe are known as sample.

(37) Schedule: Schedule is the name usually applied to a set of questions which are asked and filled in by the investigator in a face to face situation with another person.

(38) Scientific orientation: Scientific orientation means broadening the outlook of the people so that they may think logically and rationally and utilizes the scientific knowledge properly in agriculture replacing the outdated and irrelevant practices by advance techniques.

(39) Significance: Significance has two basic dimensions namely statistical significance and psychological significance. Statistical significance indicates whether the obtained results are common or rare event, if only chance is operating. Psychological significance indicates qualities of data, adequacy of the data obtained and the clarity of the obtained results.

(40) Size of land holding: It refers to the possession of land in hectares/acres by the respondents.

(41) Social participation: Degree of involvement of individual in a social organization as a member or as a office bearer.

(42) Socio-economic profile: It is the profile of socio-economic components that refer to the status of individual, group, society or organization in varying degrees. In present study, it refers to the socio-economic status of the respondents they possess.

(43) Source of information: It refers to the objects through which respondents got information about package or practices, activities about potato farming.

(44) Standard deviation: A measure of dispersion which is square root of the sum of squared deviations of each score from the mean divided by the number of scores.

(45) Technology: It is the tangible and intangible outcome of science being used facilities/by the user and consequently attaining the benefits.

(46) Variables: A variable is the description of the characteristics of a group of individuals which when measured can present more than one numerical value. Variables are of two types as follows-

(i) **Dependent variables:** The vaiables whose value is influence or is to be predicated is called dependent variables.

(ii) **Independent variables:** The variables manipulated by the experimenters for the purpuse of determining wheather it influences behaviour.

Chapter-V
RESULTS AND DISCUSSION

The findings drawn regarding the specific objectives of the study through analysis of using relevant statistical techniques have been presented in this chapter.

The findings have been divided into following subheads:

5.1: The socio-economic profile of students.

5.2: The knowledge extent of students about mass media.

5.3: The utilization pattern of mass media by the students.

5.4: The relationship between independents variable with those of dependents variable.

5.5: To assess the constraints in utilization of mass media by the students and suggestions to overcome the constraints.

5.1: The socio-economic profile of students in this section data regarding personal student's profile viz. Age, Caste, Marital status, Land holding, Family type, Family size, Material possession, Social participation, Annual family income, Extension contact, Scientific orientation, Parent occupation, House hold material, Farm power, Agriculture implements, Communication media possession, Parent total land holding , the result have been presented in subsequence tables.

Age composition:

On the basis of their age, the respondents were classified into three categories. i.e. up to 21years, 22 to 25 years, and above 26 years are as age.

Table- 5.1.1 Distribution of respondents according to their age.

N=197

S. No.	Categories (years)	Respondents	
		F	%
1.	Up to 21 years	45.00	22.84
2.	22 to 25 years	95.00	48.22
3.	26 years and above	57.00	28.94
	Total	197.0	100.00

Mean= 23.19, S.D= 2.003489, Min.= 20, Max.= 27

It reveals from the Table 5.1.1 that the maximum number of respondents (48.22%) were observed in the categories of 22 to 25 years age followed by above 26 years age is (28.94%) and up to 21 years age is (22.84%), respectively. It can be concluded that the maximum numbers of respondents were found in 22 to 25 years age.

Caste composition:

On the basis of their caste respondents were classified in to five categories i.e. General Caste, OBC Caste, SC Caste, ST Caste, and Minority.

Table-5.1.2 Distribution of respondents according to their caste.

N=197

S. No.	Categories	Respondents	
		F	%
1.	General Caste	65.00	32.99
2.	Other Backward Caste	55.00	27.93
3.	Scheduled Caste	42.00	21.32
4.	Scheduled Tribes Caste	09.00	4.57
5.	Minority	26.00	13.19
	Total	197.0	100.00

The Table 5.1.2 indicates that the maximum number of respondents were found in the general caste (32.99%) followed by Other Backward Caste (27.93%), Scheduled caste (21.32%), Minority (13.19%) and Scheduled Tribes Cast (4.57%), respectively. It can be concluded that the maximum numbers of respondents were found general caste.

Marital status:

On the basis of their marital status of respondents they were classified in to two categories. i.e. married, unmarried.

Table-5.1.3 Distribution of respondents according to their marital status.

N= 197

S. No.	Categories	Respondents	
		F	%
1.	Married	48.00	24.36
2.	Unmarried	149.0	75.64
	Total	197.0	100.00

Mean= 0.15, S.D= 0.357967, Min.= 0, Max.= 1

The Table 5.1.3 indicates that the maximum numbers of the respondents were found in unmarried (75.64%) and married respondents (24.36%) respectively. It can be concluded that the maximum numbers of respondents were found unmarried.

Table- 5.1.4 Distribution of respondents according to their family type.

On the basis of their family type of respondents they were classified in to two categories. i.e. joint family, nuclear/single family.

N=197

S. No.	Categories	Respondents	
		F	%
1.	Joint family	84.00	42.63
2.	Nuclear/ Single family	113.0	57.37
	Total	197.0	100.00

Mean= 1.105, S.D=0.307323, Min.= 1, Max.= 2

The Table 5.1.4 indicates that the maximum numbers of the respondents were found in Nuclear/Single family system (57.37%), while remaining (42.63%) respondents were observed in joint family system, respectively. It can be concluded that the maximum numbers of respondents were found in nuclear/single family.

Table- 5.1.5 Distribution of respondents according to their family size.

On the basis of their family size of respondents they were classified in to three categories. i.e. small family, medium family and large family.

N=197

S. No.	Categories (members)	Respondents	
		F	%
1.	Small (up to 4)	104.0	52.79
2.	Medium (5-8)	52.00	26.39
3.	Large (9 and above)	41.0	20.82
	Total	197	100.00

Mean= 5.675, S.D= 2.0731432, Min.= 3, Max.= 15

The Table 5.1.5 shows that the (52.79%) respondents belong to the category of those small up to 4 members in their families. 26.39% to the category of medium 5 to 8 members and 20.82% large family 9 and above members, respectively. The maximum number of respondents (52.79%) belong to the small family up to 4 members; it means that the area of study was exploded with population.

Table- 5.1.6 Distribution of respondents according to their total land holding (ha.) it parent are farmer.

On the basis of their total land holding of parent, respondents they were classified in to four categories. i.e. marginal farmer, small farmer, medium farmer and large farmer.

N= 197

S. No.	Categories (hectares)	Respondents	
		F	%
1.	Marginal (Less than 1)	32.00	16.24
2.	Small farmers (1-2)	113.0	57.36
3.	Medium farmers (3-4)	38.00	19.28
4.	Large farmers (Above 4)	14.00	7.12
	Total	197.0	100.00

Mean= 2.64015, S.D=1.412858, Min.= 0.12, Max.= 6.23

The Table-5.1.6 indicates that most of the respondents 57.36% were found in the land holding category as small (1-2 ha), followed by 19.28% in the category of medium (3-4 ha), 16.24% in the category of marginal (less than 1 ha), and 7.12% in the category of large (Above 4), respectively.

Thus, it may be said that is respondents parent small farmers categories are more than others in the study area. It seems because of fragmentation of land as a result of deviation of families.

Table- 5.1.7 Distribution of respondents according to their material possession at home.

A. Household material:

On the basis of their house hold material respondent were answers on some necessary things.

N=197

S. No.	Household material	Respondents	
		F	%
1.	Double Bed	45.00	22.84
2.	Sofa Set	18.00	9.13
3.	Dining Table	15.00	7.61

4.	Dressing Table	70.00	35.53
5.	Gas Stove with Gas Cylinder	190.0	96.44
6.	Electric Press	145.0	73.60
7.	Smokeless Stove	12.00	6.09
8.	Pressure Cooker	185.0	93.90
9.	Chair	189.0	95.93
10.	Fan	195.0	98.98
11.	Cooler	122.0	61.92
12.	Solar light	40.00	20.30
13.	Heater	62.0	31.47
14.	Cots	197.0	100.00
15.	Sewing machine	175.0	88.83
16.	Wall watch	162.0	82.23
17.	Induction Chula	48.00	24.36
18.	Almari	56.00	28.42
19.	Air-Conditioner (A.C)	09.00	4.56
20.	Electric ketli	16.00	8.12

Note: More than one items have been shown by respondent, hence the total percentage of all items would be more than 197.

Table 5.1.7 clearly indicates that the maximum number of respondents were found cots (100.00%), followed by fan (98.98%), Gas stove with Gas cylinder (96.44%), chair (95.93%), pressure cooker (93.90%), Sewing machine (88.83%), wall watch (82.23%), electric press (73.60%), cooler (61.92%), dressing table (35.53%), heater (31.47%), almari (28.42%), induction Chula (24.36%), double bed (22.84%), solar light (20.30%), sofa set (9.13%), electric Ketli (8.12%), dining table (7.61%), smokeless stove (6.09%), and Air-Conditioner (4.56%), respectively. Materials seem to be good the condition of house hold.

Table- 5.1.8 Distribution of respondents according to their communication and media possession.

On the basis of their communication and media possession respondent were answers on some necessary things.

N=197

S.N.	Communication media possession	Respondents	
		F	%
1.	T.V./ L.C.D	190.0	96.44
2.	Radio	08.00	4.06
3.	Mobile/Cell phone	197.0	100.00
4.	Telephone	05.00	2.53
5.	Tape-recorder	42.00	21.31
6.	Agricultural journals	64.00	32.48
7.	Agricultural Magazines	167.0	84.77
8.	D.T.H	185.0	93.90
9.	V.C.D/D.V.D player	15.00	7.61
10.	Agriculture books	197.0	100.00
11.	News paper	188.0	95.43
12.	Internet	192.0	97.47
13.	Desktop	56.00	28.42
14.	Laptop	143.0	72.58
15.	Printers	79.00	40.10
16.	Tablet	12.00	6.09

Note: More than one items have been shown by respondent, hence the total percentage of all items would be more than 197.

Table 5.1.8 clearly indicate that the majority of (100%), respondents were observes possessing mobile Phone and agriculture books with them. The rest of respondents who had other communication media were in descending order as Internet (97.47), T.V/L.C.D. (96.44%), newspaper (95.43%), D.T.H. (93.90%), agriculture magazine (84.77%), laptop (72.58%), printer (40.10%), agricultural journal (32.48%), desktop (28.42%), tape-recorder

(21.31%), V.C.D./DVD player (7.61%), tablet (6.09%), radio (4.06%), and telephone (2.53%), respectively. Thus, it can be inferred that mobile phone and agriculture book were main sources for getting information's and recreation purposes.

Table- 5.1.9 Distribution of respondents according to their farm power.

On the basis of their farm power respondent were answers on some necessary things.

N=197

S.N.	Farm power	Respondents	
		F	%
1.	Tractor	92.00	46.70
2	Power tiller	75.00	38.07
3	Diesel engine	152.0	77.15
4	Electronic motor	118.0	59.89
5	Tube-well	88.00	44.67
6	Solar energy pump	12.00	6.09
7	Electronic grinder	62.00	31.47

Note: More than one items have been shown by respondent, hence the total percentage of all items would be more than 197.

Table 5.1.9 Indicate that the maximum number (77.15%), of respondents having their diesel engine, followed by Electronic motor (59.89%), tractor (46.70%), tube well (44.67%), power tiller (38.07%), electronic grinder (31.47%), and solar energy pump (6.09%), respectively.

Table- 5.1.10 Distribution of respondents according to their agriculture implements.

On the basis of their agriculture implements respondent were answers on some necessary things.

N=197

S. No.	Agriculture implements	Respondents	
		F	%
1.	Desi Plough	52.00	26.39

2.	Cultivator	92.00	46.70
3.	Disc Plough	88.00	44.67
4.	Seed Drill	80.00	40.60
5.	Rotavator	75.00	38.07
6.	Cane Cutter Planter	32.00	16.24
7.	Chaff Cutter	182.0	92.38
8.	Combine Harvester	13.00	6.59
9.	Thresher	85.00	43.14
10.	Cane Crusher	98.00	49.74
11.	Leveler	89.00	45.17
12.	Sprayer	112.0	56.85
13.	Duster	35.00	17.76
14.	Kudal	167.0	84.77
15.	Shovel	155.0	78.68
16.	Khurpi	197.0	100.00
17.	Sickle	190.0	96.44
18.	Pata	99.00	50.25

Note: More than one items have been shown by respondent, hence the total percentage of all items would be more than 197.

Table 5.1.10 showed that a majority of respondents (100%) was reported having khurpi followed by sickle (96.44%), chaff cutter (92.38%), kudal (84.77%), shovel (78.68%), sprayer (56.85%), pata (50.25%), cane crusher (49.74%), cultivator (46.70%), leveler (45.17%), disc plough (44.67%), thresher (43.14%), seed drill (40.60%), rotavator (38.07%), desi plough (26.39%), duster (17.76%), cane cutter planter (16.24%), combine harvester (6.59%), respectively.

Table- 5.1.11 Distribution of respondents according to their social participation.

On the basis of their social participation respondent were answers on some necessary things.

N=197

S. No.	Participation	Respondents	
		F	%
1.	No participation	98.00	49.74
2.	Participation in one organizations	60.00	30.45
3.	Participation in two organizations	24.00	12.18
4.	Participation in more than two organizations	15.00	7.63
	Total	197.0	100.00

Mean= 0.18, S.D=0.564974, Min.= 0, Max.= 3

The Table-5.1.11 indicates that the overwhelming majority *i.e.* 30.45% of the respondents participates in one organization followed by 49.74% respondents did not take participation in any organization followed by 12.18% respondents participate in two organizations and 7.63% respondents participate in more than two organization respectively. It means that the respondents did have more interest in participating in the social organization.

Table- 5.1.12 Distribution of respondents according to parent occupation.

On the basis of their parent occupation respondent were answers on some necessary things

N=197

S. No.	Occupation	Main		Subsidiary	
		No.	%	No.	%
1.	Agriculture labor	04	2.03	07	3.55
2.	Caste based occupation	09	4.57	13	6.59
3.	Services	23	11.68	19	9.64

4.	Agriculture	138	70.05	59	29.95
5.	Business	08	4.06	27	13.70
6.	Agro based enterprise	15	7.61	23	11.69
	Total	197	100.00	148	75.12

Note: More than one items have been shown by respondent, hence the total percentage of all items would be more than 197.

It is evident from the Table 5.1.12 that the maximum (70.05%) respondent were observed such who had their main occupation as agriculture, (11.68%) service, (7.61%) Agro based enterprise, (4.57%) Caste based occupation, (4.06%) business and (2.03%) agriculture labor, respectively. The maximum (29.95%) respondent were observed such who had their subsidiary occupation as agriculture, followed by (13.70%) business, (11.69%) Agro based enterprise, (9.64%) service, (6.59%) Caste based occupation, and (3.55%) agriculture labor, respectively. On the basis of data, it can be said that agriculture is the main occupation of student's parents.

Table- 5.1.13. Distribution of the respondents according to their annual family income (Rs.).

On the basis of their annual family income respondents were be classified in to three categories, i.e. small (up to 40000), medium (40001 to 100000), high (100001 and above)

N=197

S. No.	Annual family income	Respondents	
		F	%
1.	Small (up to 40000)	52.00	26.39
2.	Medium (40001- 100000)	98.00	49.74
3.	High (100001 and above)	47.00	23.87
	Total	197.0	100.00

Mean= 76535, S.D=0.36793, Min.= 36000, Max.= 240000

The Table 5.1.13 reveals that a maximum number of the respondents 49.79% belong to the annual income Rs. 40001 to 100000 where as 26.39% and 23.87%, respondents belong to income range from up to 40000 and Rs. 100001 and above, respectively.

It can be said that the maximum respondent was having the annual income Rs. 40001-100000

5.1.14. Distribution of the respondents according to their hosing pattern.

On the basis of their housing pattern respondents were be classified in to four categories, i.e. kachcha, mixed, pucca, and hut.

N= 197

S. No.	Housing pattern	Respondents	
		F	%
1.	Kachcha	12.00	6.09
2.	Mixed	84.00	42.63
3.	Pucca	98.00	49.74
4.	Hut	03.00	1.54
	Total	197.0	100.00

Mean= 1.93, S.D= 0.255787, Min.= 1, Max.= 2

The Table 5.1.14 indicates that (49.74%) respondents reported having pucca type houses followed by, (42.63%) mixed houses, (6.09%) Kachcha house and (1.54%) huts, respectively. It means that this area was having pucca type of housing pattern.

Table- 5.1.15: Distribution of respondents according to their extension contact.

N=197

S. No.	Source of information	Respondents	
		MPS	Ranks
A.	**Formal source**		
1.	B.D.O.	0.12	VIII
2.	A.D.Os	0.11	X
3.	V.D.Os	0.27	III
4.	Kisan Sahayak	0.15	VI
5.	Gram-Pradhan	0.25	IV
6.	Co-operative	0.13	IX
7.	Agril.College/ University/Institute	6.12	I
8.	Mandi Samiti	0.14	VII
9.	Fertilizers/Seed stores agencies	0.18	V
10.	Agril.Scientists	6.04	II
	Average	**1.35**	
B.	**Informal source**		
1.	Family Members	3.00	III
2.	Neighbors	6.10	II
3.	Friends	6.13	I
4.	Relatives	1.08	VI
5.	Local leaders	1.10	V
6.	Progressive farmers	2.94	IV
	Average	**3.39**	
C.	**Mass media contact**		
1.	Radio	0.18	XII
2.	T.V. /L.C.D	6.10	V
3.	News paper	6.13	III
4.	Agril. Books	6.11	IV

5.	News bulletin	6.09	VI
6.	Farm magazines	2.91	IX
7.	Circular letter	0.10	XVI
8.	Poster	3.17	VIII
9.	Mobiles/Cell phone	6.15	I
10.	Famers Fair	0.12	XV
11.	Demonstration	0.14	XIV
12.	Film shows	0.23	XI
13.	Exhibitions	0.16	XIII
14.	Internet	6.14	II
15.	Desktop/Laptop	5.69	VII
16.	General magazines	0.33	X
	Average	**3.90**	
	Overall average:	**8.641**	

Mean= 80.815, S.D= 2.292828, Min.= 76, Max.= 92

Table 5.1.15 shows the extent of contact of respondents with different information sources as used by them for general information as well as about various extension contact sources. The information sources were categorized into three categories namely, formal sources, informal sources and mass media contact to find out the extension contact of respondents. In case of formal sources ranks i.e. Agril. College/ university/ institute I^{st}, Agril. Scientist IInd, V.D.O IIIrd, Gram pradhan IVth, Fertilizers/ seed storage agencies V^{th}, Kisan sahayak VIth, Mandi samiti VIIth, B.D.O. VIIIth Co-operative IXth and A.D.Os. X^{th}, respectively.

So for as informal sources like ranks i.e. Friends I^{st}, Neighbors IInd, Family members IIIrd, Progressive farmer IVth, Local leader V^{th}, Relative VIth, respectively.

So for as mass media source like was found in ranks i.e. Mobile phone I^{st}, Internet IInd, Newspapers IIIrd, Agril. Books IVth, T.V./L.C.D. V^{th}, News buletien VIth, Desktop/ leptop VIIth, Posters VIIIth, Farm magazines IXth, General magazines X^{th}, Film shows

XIth, Radio XIIth, Exibition XIIIth, Demostration XIVth, Farmer fair XVth, and Circular letter XVIth respectively.

Table- 5.1.16: Distribution of respondents according to general knowledge about mobile mass media pattern.

N=197

S. No.	Knowledge about mobile mass media pattern	Respondents	
		MPS	Ranks
A.	Function of mobile mass media pattern		
1.	Call for other	2.01	I
2.	Receive call other	1.20	II
3.	Whatsapp message	1.09	IV
4.	Audio chat	1.11	III
5.	E-mail	0.95	X
6.	Mobile touch	0.98	IX
7.	Calculator	0.99	VIII
8.	Watch	1.08	V
9.	Multimedia	1.07	VI
10.	News	0.94	XI
11.	Facebook	0.90	XIV
12.	Google	0.92	XIII
13.	SMS (Sort Message Services)	1.02	VII
14.	Twitter	0.93	XII
15.	IMO	0.65	XVI
16.	Others	0.78	XV
	Average	1.08	
B.	Recharge top up senses		
1.	Top up	0.90	VII
2.	Recharge	1.11	II
3.	Internet pack	1.12	I

4.	Tariff	1.01	III
5.	Validity recharge	0.97	IV
6.	SMS pack	0.98	V
7.	Others	0.92	VI
	Average	**1.00**	
C.	**Recharge provider company**		
1.	BSNL	1.12	IV
2.	Reliance	1.20	**III**
3.	Vodafone	1.23	**II**
4.	Jio	1.40	**I**
5.	Airtel	1.09	V
6.	Idea	0.99	VI
7.	Tata docomo	0.90	VIII
8.	Telenor	0.98	VII
9.	Others	0.78	IX
	Average	**1.07**	
D.	**Mobile mass media pattern provider Company**		
1.	LG	0.97	IX
2.	Lava	0.75	X
3.	Nokia	0.71	XI
4.	korbon	0.29	XII
5.	HTC	0.99	VIII
6.	Micromax	1.11	V
7.	Oppo	1.12	IV
8.	Lenovo	1.09	VI
9.	Samsung	6.40	**I**
10.	Xiomi	1.23	**III**
11.	Vivo	6.04	**II**
12.	Gionee	1.08	VII

13.	Others	023	XIII
	Average	**3.44**	
E	**Which is used network about mobile mass media pattern?**		
1.	Vodaphone	1.20	II
2.	Jio	1.34	I
3.	Airtel	0.99	III
4.	Idea	0.98	IV
5.	BSNL	0.95	V
6.	Reliance	0.25	VI
7.	Others	0.11	VII
	Average	**0.83**	
F	**Who is used of mobile mass media pattern?**		
1.	Key pad mobile phone	0.34	II
2.	Android mobile	0.99	I
	Average	**0.66**	
	Overall Average	**8.08**	

Table 5.1.16 Show that the among all information related to the general knowledge of mobile mass media utilization pattern uses by the respondents, and the all information sources were categorized in to six category, namely function of mobile mass media pattern, recharge top up senses, recharge provider company, mobile mass media pattern provider company, which is used network about mobile mass media pattern?, who is used of mobile mass media pattern?. The first categories ranks as for a s namely, call for other I^{st}, receive call other IInd, audio chat IIIrd, whatsapp message IVth, watch V^{th}, multimedia VIth, SMS (Sort Message Services) VIIth, calculator VIIIth, mobile tuch IXth, E-mail X^{th}, News XIth, Twitter XIIth, Google XIIIth, Facebook XIVth, Other XVth, IMO XVIth, respectively

Second categories ranks as for as namely, internet pack I^{st}, recharge IInd, tariff IIIrd, validity recharge IVth, SMS pack V^{th}, other VIth, and top up VIIth, respectively.

Third categories ranks as for as namely, Jio I^{st}, vodaphone IInd, reliance IIIrd, BSNL IVth, aritel V^{th}, idea VIth, telenor VIIth, tatadocomo VIIIth, and other IXth, respectively

Fourth categories ranks as for as namely, sumsung I^{st}, vivo IInd, xiomi IIIrd, oppo IVth, micrimax V^{th}, lenovo VIth, gionee VIIth, HTC VIIIth, LG IXth, lava X^{th}, noki XIth, korbon XIIth, and other XIIIth, respectively.

Fifth categories ranks as for as namely, jio I^{st}, vodaphone IInd, aritel IIIrd, idea IVth, BSNL V^{th}, reliance VIth, other VIIth, respectively.

Six categories ranks as for as namely, android mobile I^{st}, key pad mobile IInd, respectively.

Scientific orientation:

Table- 5.1.17. Distribution of the respondents according to their scientific orientation.

On the basis of their scientific orientation respondents were be classified in to three categories, i.e. low (up to 35), medium (36 to 44), and high (above 44).

N=197

S. No.	Categories (score value)	Respondents	
		F	%
1	low (up to 41),	50.00	25.38
2	medium (42 to 44)	85.00	43.14
3	high (45 and above).	62.00	31.48
	Total	197.0	100.00

Mean= 42.42, S.D= 1.55, Min.= 38, Max.= 47

Table 5.1.17 it was found that the maximum number of respondents (43.14%) was found having medium level of scientific orientation while (31.48%) high and (25.38%) respondents were found in the categories of low scientific orientation each, respectively.

5.2: The knowledge extent of students about mass media.

Table-5.2.1. Distribution of the respondents according to their knowledge extent about mass media utilization pattern:

N=197

Results and Discussion

S. No.	Knowledge Extent	Respondents	
		MPS	Ranks
A.	**Have you know of mass media pattern?**		
1.	Radio	0.99	VI
2.	Television/ L.C.D	1.06	II
3.	Laptop/Computer	1.01	V
4.	Newspaper	1.03	IV
5.	Agril. Books	1.04	III
6.	Journals /Agril. magazines	0.94	X
7.	Mobiles/Cell phone/Android phone	1.10	I
8.	Demonstration	0.96	IX
9.	Film shows	0.88	XII
10.	Exhibitions	0.98	VII
11.	Posters	0.90	XI
12.	Leaflets	0.87	XIII
13.	Pumlets	0.97	VIII
14.	Folders	0.78	XIV
15.	Charts	0.72	XV
	Average	1.58	
B.	**Do you have knowledge about the following function of mass media pattern?**		
1	Proper channel provide for mass communication	0.92	IV
2	Internet	0.87	V
3	Email	0.94	III
4	To use the social network (e.g.Google/Facebook /wathsapp/academic.edu. etc.)	0.86	VI
5	New information collection and spread	0.96	I
6	Provide technical knowledge	0.95	II
	Average	0.91	
C.	**Do you know about the following services of mass media pattern?**		

1	Internet services	1.01	II
2	Entertainment services	1.80	I
3	Give new information related services	0.89	V
4	Help in the research services	0.73	VI
5	Transfer/ Transaction services	0.90	IV
6	Communication services	0.99	III
	Average	1.05	
D	Do you know about the agency/Institutes which, provides need information related to agriculture development and its allied viz. Dairy, Fisheries, Agro-forestry, Horticulture, Agricultural Extension etc. through mass media pattern?		
1	Kisan Call Centers provides information to students through direct contact through different mass media pattern.	1.10	II
2	ATICs (Agriculture Technology Information Centre)	1.11	I
3	Krishi Vigyan Kendras (KVKs)	0.99	III
4	Agriculture Department	0.84	V
5	NGOs	0.67	VI
6	Private agencies	0.98	IV
	Average	0.94	
E	Do you know about following specific information needed about your better future through mass media pattern?		
1	Information for better develop new strategies	1.01	I
2	Information about research work	0.99	II
3	New information for develop the management practices	0.98	III
4	Information about for change technology knowledge	0.95	IV
	Average	0.98	
F	Which, services known by the student's group via mass media pattern?		

1	AGRISNET (Agricultural Informatics and Communication System Network)	0.96	VI
2	AQUA (Almost Questions Answered)	0.65	VII
3	AGMARKNET (Agricultural Marketing Information System)	0.95	VIII
4	Research work	1.11	II
5	Facebook	0.98	V
6	Chatting	0.99	IV
7	Whatsapp	1.23	I
8	e-market plus	1.02	III
9	e-Governance	0.78	IX
10	e-Choupal	0.63	X
	Average	**0.93**	
G	**What benefits/advantages do you know from using mass media pattern in communicating information?**		
1	Help to easily send or communicate information anytime the need arose	1.22	II
2	Mostly solve problem quickly	0.78	VI
3	Assist in obtaining new information quickly	0.85	V
4	Help to exchange new information anytime the need arose	1.23	I
5	Increase technology knowledge of students quickly	0.95	III
6	Continuous helps in accumulate current information from accruing area	0.93	IV
	Average	**0.99**	
	Overall average	**7.38**	

Mean= 110.295, S.D= 4.660103, Min.= 88, Max.= 123

Table 5.2.1 Show that the among all of mass media utilization pattern by the respondents extent of knowledge, and general information sources as well as about various knowledge on mass media utilization pattern. The all information sources were categorized in to seven category, namely Have you know of mass media pattern?, Do you have knowledge about the following function of mass media pattern?, Do you know about the following services of mass media pattern, Do you know about the agency/ Institutes which, provides need information related to agriculture development and its allied viz. Dairy, Fisheries, Agro-forestry, Horticulture, Agricultural Extension etc. through mass media pattern?, Do you know about following specific information needed about your better future through mass media pattern?, Which, services known by the student's group via mass media pattern?, What benefits/advantages do you know from using mass media pattern in communicating information?. The first categories ranks at were concerned like mobile/ cell phone/android phone I^{st}, television/L,C.D IInd, agril. books IIIrd, newspapers IVth, laptop/computer V^{th}, radio VIth, exibitions VIIth, pumplets VIIIth, demostration IXth, journals/agril. magazines X^{th}, posters XIth, film shows XIIth, leaflets XIIIth, folders XIVth, and charts XVth, respectively.

Second categories ranks were concerned like new information collection and spread I^{st}, provide technical knowledge IInd, email IIIrd, proper channel provide for mass communication IVth, internet V^{th}, and to use the social network VIth, respectively.

Third categories ranks were concerned like entertainment service I^{st}, internet sevice IInd, communication service IIIrd, transfer/ transaction service IVth, give new information related services V^{th}, and help in the research service VIth, respectively.

Fourth categories ranks were concerned like ATICs (Agriculture Technology Information Centre) I^{st}, Kisan Call Centers provides information to students through direct contact through different mass media pattern provide technical knowledge IInd, Krishi Vigyan Kendras (KVKs) IIIrd, Private agencies IVth, Agriculture department V^{th}, and NGOs VIth, respectively.

Fifth categories ranks were concerned like Information for better develop new strategies I^{st}, Information about research work IInd, New information for develop the management practices IIIrd, and Information about for change technology knowledge IVth, respectively.

Results and Discussion

Six categories ranks were concerned like Whatsapp Ist, research work IInd, e-market plus IIIrd, chatting IVth, facebook Vth, AGRISNET (Agricultural Informatics and Communication System Network) VIth, AQUA (Almost Questions Answered) VIIth, AGMARKNET (Agricultural Marketing Information System) VIIIth, e-Governace IXth, and e-Choupal Xth, respectively.

Seventh categories ranks were concerned like Help to exchange new information anytime the need arose Ist, Help to easily send or communicate information anytime the need arose IInd, Increase technology knowledge of students quickly IIIrd, Continuous helps in accumulate current information from accruing area IVth, Assist in obtaining new information quickly Vth, and Mostly solve problem quickly VIth, respectively.

Table-5.2.2. Distribution of the respondents according to their knowledge extent about educational atmosphere in your university related to mass media utilization pattern:

N=197

S. No.	Knowledge Extent	Respondents	
		MPS	Ranks
1.	Teaching through projector	0.96	III
2	Research work show through projector	0.97	II
3	ATIC	0.95	IV
4	Library	0.99	I
5	Demonstration of field research trial	0.94	V
	Average	0.96	

Table 5.2.2 Show that the among all of mass media utilization pattern users by the respondents extent of knowledge about educational atmosphere in his university, and general information sources as well as about various knowledge on mass media utilization pattern. The all information sources were concerned like Library Ist, Research work show through projector IInd, teaching through projector IIIrd, ATIC IVth, and Demonstration of field research trial Vth, respectively.

Table- 5.2.3 Distribution of the respondents according to their knowledge extent about contact with information sources in your university:

N=197

S. No.	Source of information	Respondents	
		MPS	Ranks
A.	**Formal source**		
1.	Vic-chancellor of university	0.93	VIII
2.	Dean of college	0.95	VI
3.	Advisor	1.21	I
4.	Major member	1.11	II
5.	Placement officer	0.65	X
6.	Hostel warden	0.99	IV
7.	Registrar	0.94	VII
8.	Deputy registrar	0.76	IX
9.	Head of the department	1.10	III
10.	Other teacher	0.98	V
11.	Teacher of the other university	0.64	XI
12.	Any others	0.62	XII
	Average	**0.90**	

Table 5.2.3 Show that the among respondents extent of knowledge, and general information sources as well as contact in his university various knowledge on mass media utilization pattern. The all information sources were concerned, namely formal sources rank like Advisor Ist, Major member IInd, Head of the department IIIrd, Hostel warden IVth, other teacher Vth, Dean of college VIth, Registrar VIIth, Vic-chancellor of university VIIIth, Deputy registrar IXth, Placement officer Xth, Teacher of other universty XIth, and Any other XIIth, respectively.

5.3: The utilization pattern of mass media by the students:

Table- 5.3.1 Distribution of respondents according to their mass media utilization pattern for the collection of information.

On the basis of their uses of mass media utilization pattern respondent were answers on some necessary things.

N=197

S. No.	Mass media utilization pattern	Respondents	
		F	%
A.	Radio:		
1.	News	80.00	40.60
2.	Agriculture information	42.00	21.32
3.	Entertainment	55.00	27.93
4.	Course study	20.00	10.15
	Total	197.0	100.00
B.	Television:		
1.	News	95.00	48.22
2.	Entertainment	25.00	12.69
3.	Sport news	55.00	27.91
4.	Discovery/ wild life news	12.00	6.09
5.	Movies	10.00	5.09
	Total	197.0	100.00
C.	Laptop/ Computer:		
1.	Entertainment	50.00	25.38
2.	Internet	30.00	15.22
3	Playing game	10.00	5.07
4.	Research work	55.00	27.91
5.	Data analysis & collection	35.00	17.78
6.	News	17.00	8.64

		Total	197.0	100.00
D.	**Newspaper:**			
1.	National news		75.00	38.07
2.	State news		45.00	22.84
3.	Local news		25.00	12.69
4.	World news		32.00	16.24
5.	Sports news		20.00	10.16
		Total	197.0	100.00
E	**Agril. Books.**			
1.	Preparation		95.00	48.22
2.	Reading		25.00	12.69
3.	Agriculture practices managements		10.00	5.07
4.	Knowledge		22.00	11.16
5.	Only course examination		45.00	22.86
		Total	197.0	100.00
F.	**Magazines:**			
1.	Farm management information		50.00	25.38
2.	Animal husbandry development information		45.00	22.84
3.	Poultry development information		20.00	10.15
4.	Farming development information		25.00	12.69
5.	Preparation for the competitive exams		35.00	17.76
6.	Entertainment		22.00	11.18
		Total	197.0	100.00
G	**Mobile/ cell phone/Android phone :**			
1.	News		10.00	5.07
2.	Entertainment		25.00	12.69
3.	Communication		95.00	48.22
4.	Internet		57.00	28.95
5.	Search abstract and topic		6.00	3.04

6.		Competitive examination	04.00	2.03
		Total	197.0	
H.	**Demonstration:**			
1.		Sowing new practice for student development	85.00	43.14
2.		Sowing new technical information	45.00	22.84
3.		Build confidence about student	22.00	11.17
4.		Motivation and stimulate student for action	30.00	15.23
5.		Improving knowledge	15.00	7.62
		Total	197.0	100.00
I.	**Film shows:**			
1.		Transfer of new technology	80.00	40.61
2.		Transfer new method for managing farm	55.00	27.92
3.		Receive information	42.00	21.32
4.		Entertainment	20.00	10.15
		Total	197.0	10.00
J.	**Exhibitions:**			
1.		Education	82.00	41.62
2.		Skill development	48.00	24.36
3.		Attitude development	32.00	16.25
4.		Change behavior	35.00	17.77
		Total	197.0	100.00
K	**Posters:**			
1.		Quick display knowledge gain	32.00	16.24
2.		Fast receiving message	35.00	17.77
3.		Display of awareness in class room	85.00	43.15
4.		Display of technical information in class room	45.00	22.84
		Total	197.0	100.00

Note: More than one items have been shown by respondent, hence the total percentage of all items would be more than 197.

Table 5.3.1 which is reveals that the usage of mass media utilization pattern to different purpose by the respondents, general information as well as development the of students about mass media utilization pattern, namely Radio, Television, Laptop/Computer, Newspapers, Agril. Books, Magazines, Mobiles/Cell phone/Android phone, Demonstration, Film show, Exhibition, and Posters. The respondents use different purpose.

So far radio mass media utilization pattern source, shows that the majority of respondents (40.60%), was reported having news, followed by entertainment (27.93%), agriculture information (21.32%), and course study (10.15%), respectively.

So far television mass media utilization pattern source, shows that the majority of respondents (48.22%), was reported having news, followed by sport news (27.91%), entertainment (12.69%), discovery/wild life news (6.09%), and movies (5.09%), respectively.

So far laptop/computer mass media utilization pattern source, shows that the majority of respondents (27.91%), was reported having research work, followed by entertainment (25.38%), data analysis & collection (17.78%), internet (15.22%), news (8.64%), and playing game (5.07%), respectively.

So far newspaper mass media utilization pattern source, shows that the majority of respondents (38.07%), was reported having national news, followed by state news (22.84%), world news (16.24%), local news (12.69%), and sport news (10.16), respectively.

So far agril. books mass media utilization pattern source, shows that the majority of respondents (48.22%), was reported having preparation, followed by only course examination (22.86%), reading (12.69%), knowledge (11.16%), and agriculture practices managements (5.07%), respectively.

So far magazines mass media utilization pattern source, shows that the majority of respondents (25.38%), was reported having farm management information, followed by animal husbandry development information (22.84%), preparation for the competitive exams (17.76%), farming development (12.69%), entertainment (11.18%), and poultry development information (10.15%), respectively.

So far mobile/cell phone/ android phone mass media utilization pattern source, shows that the majority of respondents (48.22%), was reported having communication, followed by internet (28.95%), entertainment (12.69%), news (5.07%), search abstract & topic (3.04%), and competitive examination (2.03%), respectively

So far demonstration mass media utilization pattern source, shows that the majority of respondents (43.14%), was reported having Sowing new practice for student development, followed by Sowing new technical information (22.84%), motivation and stimulate student for action (15.23%), Build confidence about student (11.17%), and improving knowledge (7.62), respectively.

So far film shows mass media utilization pattern source, shows that the majority of respondents (40.61%), was reported having transfer of new technology, followed by transfer of new method for managing farm (27.92%), receive information (21.32%), and entertainment (5.07%), respectively.

So far exhibition mass media utilization pattern source, shows that the majority of respondents (41.62%), was reported having education knowledge development, followed by skill development (24.36%), change behavior (17.77%), and attitude development (16.25%), respectively.

So far posters mass media utilization pattern source, shows that the majority of respondents (43.15%), was reported having display of awareness in classroom, followed by display of technical information in classroom (20.30%), fast receiving message (17.77%), and quick display knowledge gain (16.24%), respectively.

Statistical analysis:

5.4: Relationship between independents variable with those of dependents variable.

Table- 5.4.1 Correlation coefficient (r) between different variables and Knowledge extent about post graduate students.

N=197

S.N	Variables	Correlation coefficient
1	Age	0.004731
2	Cast	-0.0529
3	Marital status	0.205293**
4	Family type	0.164229*
5	Family Size	0.251527**
6	Land holding	0.16975*
7	Material possession	0.256765**
8	social participation	0.162959*
9	Family Income	0.252818**
10	Housing pattern	0.337806**
11	Extension contact	0.272267**
12	Scientific orientation	0.271427**

*Significant at 0.05% probability level   0.139

** Significant at 0.01% probability level   0.182

Table 5.4.1 focuses that the out of 12 variables studied, the variables marital status, family size, material possession, family income, housing pattern, extension contact, and scientific orientation highly significant and positively correlated with knowledge extent about using mass media utilization pattern, the variable like family type, land holding, and social participation, was found significant and positively correlated. The variable like age was found positively correlated with knowledge extent about using mass media utilization pattern and the variable caste only found negatively correlated with knowledge extent about using mass media utilization pattern. Those variables which showed the significant, positive and negative relationship between independents and dependence variables had direct influence overuse of knowledge extent on mass media utilization pattern by the students for his development. It means that if the values variables increase. Knowledge extent about post graduate students will also increase.

Table- 5.4.2 Correlation coefficient (r) between different variables and Knowledge extent about mass media utilization pattern to post graduate students.

N=197

S. No.	Independent Variable	Correlation
1	Age	0.073336
2	Cast	-0.02493
3	Marital status	0.126716
4	Family type	0.068108
5	Family Size	0.026424
6	Land holding	0.047789
7	Material possession	0.208658**
8	social participation	0.065748
9	Family Income	0.039197
10	Housing pattern	0.172493*
11	Extension contact	0.186338**
12	Scientific orientation	0.202309**

*Significant at 0.05% probability level   0.139

** Significant at 0.01% probability level   0.182

Table 5.4.2 focuses that the out of 12 variables studied, the variable material possession, extension contact and scientific orientation highly significant and possivelity correlated with mass media utilization pattern, the variable like housing pattern and age, marital status, family type, family size, land holding, social participation and family

Results and Discussion

income significant and highly positive correlated. The variable like caste were found negative correlated about mass media utilization pattern using by post graduate students. Those variables which showed the significant, positive and negative relationship between independents and dependence variables had direct influence overuse of knowledge extent about mass media utilization pattern by the post graduate students for his development. It means that if the values variables increase. Knowledge extent about mass media utilization pattern for post graduate students will also increase.

5.5 Constraints:

Table-5.5.1 Constraints in mass media utilization pattern perceived by the students.

On the basis of their uses of mass media utilization pattern to overcome the constraints respondent were answers on some necessary things.

N=197

S. No.	Problems/ constrains	Respondents F	%	Rank
1.	Lack of money for purchase of mass media utilization pattern	178.0	90.35	IX
2.	Lack of time for listen and seen of mass media utilization pattern for gathering information .0	135.0	68.52	XIV
3.	Lack of light for charging mass media utilization pattern equipments	187.0	94.92	VII
4.	Weak and slow networking in the university campus	195.0	98.98	II
5.	Wi-Fi facility not available in university campus	175.0	88.83	X
6.	High cost of internet package for recharging	196.0	99.49	I
7.	Spreading fake news in mobile mass media uses	162.0	82.23	XIII

8.	Problem of language when mass media utilization pattern	85.0	43.14	XVI
9.	Heavy work load in course study	170.0	86.24	XI
10.	Limited internet facilities in universities computer lab	192.0	97.46	IV
11.	Insufficient technical support	165.0	83.75	XII
12.	Proper literature is not available in the university library	189.0	95.93	VI
13.	Lack of fund within the university building for internet lab	75.0	38.07	XVII
14.	Slow data speed of internet in hostel, department, and college	190.0	96.44	V
15.	Proper not available equipment related to mass media utilization pattern	194.0	98.47	III
16.	Very price full mass media utilization pattern	183.0	92.89	VIII
17.	Lack of proper Broadcasting by the mass media utilization pattern	123.0	62.43	XV

Note: More than one items have been shown by respondent, hence the total percentage of all constrains would be more than 197.

A perusal of the Table 5.5.1 indicate out of the 17 common problem that the maximum number of the respondents (99.49%) with adopt a rank of first were agreed with the statements that high cost of internet package for recharging is the common problem, followed by weak slow networking in the university campus (98.98%) at rank second, proper not available equipment related to mass media utilization pattern (98.47%) at rank third, limited internet facilities in universities computer lab (97.46%) at rank forth, slow data speed of internet in hostel, department, and college (96.44%) at rank fifth, proper literature is not available in the university library (95.93%) at rank sixth, lack of light for charging mass media utilization pattern equipments (94.92%) at rank seventh, very price full mass media utilization pattern (92.89%) at rank eighth, lack of money for purchase of mass media utilization pattern (90.35%) at rank ninth, Wi-Fi facility not available in university campus (88.83%) at rank tenth, heavy work load in course study (86.24%) at rank eleventh, insufficient technical support (83.75%) at rank twelfth, spreading fake news in mobile mass media uses (82.23%) at rank thirteenth, lack of time for listen and seen of mass media utilization pattern for gathering information (68.52%) at rank fourteenth, lack of proper broadcasting by the mass media utilization pattern (62.43%) at rank fifteenth, problem of language when mass media utilization pattern 43.14% at rank sixteenth, and lack of fund within the university building for internet lab (38.07%) at rank seventeenth, respectively.

Suggestion:

Table-5.5.2 Suggestion in mass media utilization pattern perceived by the students.

On the basis of their uses of mass media utilization pattern to overcome the constraints respondent were answers on some necessary things.

N=197

S. No.	Suggestion	Respondents F	%	Rank
1.	Financial support for purchase of mass media utilization pattern	196.0	99.49	I
2.	Proper time given by the students for listen and seen of mass media utilization pattern for gathering information	195.0	98.98	II
3.	Proper provided light facility for charging mass med.0ia utilization pattern equipments .0	194.0	98.47	III
4.	Improving networking system in the university campus	192.0	97.46	IV
5.	Wi-Fi facility provided in university campus	190.0	96.44	V

6.	Low cost of internet package for recharging	189.0	95.93	VI
7.	Non spreading fake news in mobile mass media uses	183.0	92.89	VII
8.	Used simple language when mass media utilization pattern by the students	178.0	90.35	VIII
9.	Decreasing work load in course study.	170.0	86.29	IX
10.	Unlimited internet facilities provided by in the universities computer lab.	165.0	83.75	X
11.	Sufficient technical support.	163.0	82.74	XI
12.	Proper literature is provided by the university library.	158.0	80.20	XII
13.	Proper fund provided by the govt. to university building for internet lab.	155.0	78.68	XIII
14.	Improve networking system in hostel, department, and college.	153.0	77.64	XIV
15.	Proper available equipment related to mass media utilization pattern in university campus	150.0	76.14	XV
16.	Mass media utilization pattern available in the market low prices for purchasable about students	149.0	75.63	XVI
17.	Regular Broadcasting by the mass media utilization pattern	145.0	73.60	XVII

Note: More than one items have been shown by respondent, hence the total percentage of all constrains would be more than 197.

A perusal of the Table 5.1.2 indicate that the maximum number of the respondents 99.49 % with adopt a rank of first were agreed with the statements that financial support for purchase of mass media utilization pattern is the common suggestion, followed by proper time given by the students for listen and seen of mass media utilization pattern for gathering information (98.98%) at rank second, proper provided light facility for charging mass media utilization pattern equipments (98.47%) at rank third, improving networking system in the university campus (97.46%) at rank fourth, Wi-Fi facility provided in university campus (96.44%) at rank fifth, low cost of internet package for recharging (95.93%) at rank sixth, non spreading fake news in mobile mass media uses (92.89%) at rank seventh, used simple language when mass media utilization pattern by the students (90.35%) at rank eighth, decreasing work load in course study (86.29%) at rank ninth, unlimited internet facilities provided by in the universities computer lab (83.75%) at rank tenth, sufficient technical support (82.74%) at rank eleventh, proper literature is provided by the university library (80.20%) at rank twelfth, proper fund provided by the govt. to university building for internet lab (78.68%) at rank thirteenth, improve networking system in hostel, department, and college (77.64%) at rank fourteen, Proper available equipment related to mass media utilization pattern in university campus (76.14%) at rank fifteen, mass media utilization pattern available in the market low prices for purchasable about students (75.63%) at rank sixteen, and regular broadcasting by the mass media utilization pattern (73.60%) at rank seventeen, respectively.

Chapter-VI

SUMMARY AND CONCLUSIOS

The present study entitled **"Study on mass media utilization pattern of the Post Graduate students of agriculture in State Agriculture Universities of Uttar Pradesh."** Was under taken during the year 2018-2019 out of four agriculture universities in Utter Pradesh, all four universities and Post Graduate students of agriculture were selected for this study. Complete list of all Post graduate students were prepared a total number of 197 students selected through proportionate random sampling technique keeping in their education at categories. The investigator himself had collection of the data from the pre-tested interview schedule.

Analysis of data was done with the use of percentage as well as correlation coefficient to see the relationship between different variable and knowledge, knowledge extent find out the mass media utilization pattern uses by the Post Graduate students. The study also highlights the constraints and suggestion as perceived by the respondents in mass media utilization pattern about Post Graduate students in all four state agriculture universities namely, Acharya Narendera Deva University of Agriculture & Technology, Kumargunj, (Ayodhya), Chandera Shekhar Azad University of Agriculture& Technology, (Kanpur), Sardar vallabhbhai Patel University of Agriculture & technology, (Meerut) and Banda University of Agriculture &Technology, (Banda).

This study was conducted keeping in view of the following objective-

    1. To study the socio-economic profile of students.

    2. To study the knowledge extent of students about mass media.

    3. To study the utilization pattern of mass media by the students.

    4. To find out the relationship between independents variable with those of dependent variable.

Summary and Conclusions

5. To assess the constraints in utilization of mass media by the students and suggestions to overcome the constraints.

1. The socio-economic profile of students:

(I) The maximum number of respondents (48.22%) were observed in the categories of (22 to 25 years) age followed by (above 26 years) age is (28.94%) and (up to 21 years) age is (22.84%), and respectively.

(II) The maximum number of respondents observed in the general caste (32.99%) followed by Other Backward Caste (27.93%), Scheduled caste (21.32%), Minority (13.19%) and Scheduled Tribes Cast (4.57%), respectively.

(III) The maximum number of the unmarried respondents 75.64% and married respondents 24.36% respectively.

(IV) The maximum number of the respondents Nuclear/ Single family system 57.37%, while remaining 42.63% respondents were observed in joint family system, respectively.

(V) The majority of 52.79% respondents belong to the category of those small up to 4members in their families. 26.39 % to the category of medium 5 to 8 members, and large family 9 and above members, 20.82% respectively.

(VI) The maximum number of the respondents 57.36% were found in the land holding category as small (1-2 ha), 19.28% in the category of medium (3-4 ha), 16.24% in the category of marginal (less than 1 ha), and in the category of large (Above 4) 7.12% respectively.

(VII) The maximum number indicate that cots (100.00%), respondents were reported having cots followed by fan (98.98), and Gas stove with Gas cylinder (96.44), chair (95.93), pressure cooker (93.90), Sewing machine (88.83), wall watch (82.23), electric press (73.60), cooler (61.92), dressing table (35.53), heater (31.47), almari (28.42), induction Chula (24.36), dual bed (22.84), solar light (20.30), sofa set (9.13), electric Ketli

(8.12), dining table (7.61), smokeless stove (6.09) and Air-Conditioner (4.5 6), respectively.

(VIII) The majority of (100%), respondents were observes possessing mobile Phone and agriculture books (100%) with them. The rest of respondents who had other communication media were in descending order as Internet (97.47), T.V/L.C.D. (96.44%), newspaper (95.43%), D.T.H. (93.90%), agriculture magazine (84.77%), laptop (72.58%), printer (40.10%), agricultural journal (32.48%), desktop (28.42%), tape-recorder (21.31%), V.C.D./DVD player (7.61%), tablet (6.09%), radio (4.06%), and telephone (2.53), respectively.

(IX) The maximum number that (77.15), of respondents having their diesel engine, followed by Electronic motor (59.89), tractor (46.70), tube well (44.67), power tiller (38.07), electronic grinder (31.47), solar energy pump (6.09), respectively.

(X) The majority of respondents (100%), was reported having khurpi, followed by sickle (96.44%), chaff cutter (92.38%), kudal (84.77%), shovel (78.68%), sprayer (56.85%), pata (50.25%), cane crusher (49.74), cultivator (46.70), leveler (45.17), disc plough (44.67), thresher (43.14), seed drill (40.60), rotawater (38.07), deshi plough (26.39), duster (17.76), cane cutter planter (16.24), combine harvester (6.59), respectively.

(XI) The overwhelming majority *i.e.* 30.45% of the respondents participates in one organization followed by 49.74% respondents did not take participation in any organization, 12.18% respondents in two organizations and 7.63% respondents in more than two organization respectively. It means that the respondents did have more interest in participating in the social organization.

(XII) The maximum (70.05%) respondent were observed such who had their main occupation as agriculture, (11.68%) service, (7.61%) Agro based enterprise, (4.57%) Caste based occupation, (4.06%) business, and (2.03%) agriculture labor, respectively. The maximum (29.95%) respondent were observed such who had their subsidiary occupation as agriculture followed by (13.70%) business, (11.69%) Agro based enterprise, (9.64%) service, (6.59%) Caste based occupation, and (3.55%) agriculture labor, respectively.

Summary and Conclusions

(XIII) The maximum number of the respondents 49.79% belong to the annual income Rs. 40001 to 100000 where as 26.39% and 23.87%, respondents belong to income range from up to 40000 and Rs. 100001 and above, respectively.

(XIV) The majority of 49.74% respondents reported having pucca type houses followed by, 42.63% mixed houses, 6.09% kachcha house and 1.54% huts, respectively.

(XV) The majority of formal sources ranks i.e. Agril. College/ university/ institute I^{st}, Agril. Scientist IInd, V.D.O IIIrd, Gram pradhan IVth, Fertilizers/ seed storage agencies V^{th}, Kisan sahayak VIth, Mandi samiti VIIth, B.D.O. VIIIth Co-operative IXth and A.D.Os. X^{th}. So for as informal sources like ranks i.e. Friends I^{st}, Neighbors IInd, Family members IIIrd, Progressive farmer IVth, Local leader V^{th}, and Relative VIth. So for as mass media source like was found in ranks i.e. Mobile phone I^{st}, Internet IInd, Newspapers IIIrd, Agril. Books IVth, T.V./L.C.D. V^{th}, News buletien VIth, Desktop/ laptop VIIth, Posters VIIIth, Farm magazines IXth, General magazines X^{th}, Film shows XIth, Radio XIIth, Exhibition XIIIth, Demonstration XIVth, Farmer fair XVth, and Circular letter XVIth respectively.

(XVI) A maximum number of respondents uses mobile mass media utilization pattern first categories, call for other I^{st}, receive call other IInd, audio chat IIIrd, whatsapp message IVth, watch V^{th}, multimedia VIth, SMS (Sort Message Services) VIIth, calculator VIIIth, mobile tuch IXth, E-mail X^{th}, News XIth, Twitter XIIth, Google XIIIth, Facebook XIVth, Other XVth, and IMO XVIth. Second categories ranks as for as namely, internet pack I^{st}, recharge IInd, tariff IIIrd, validity recharge IVth, SMS pack V^{th}, other VIth, and top up VIIth. Third categories ranks as for as namely, Jio I^{st}, vodaphone IInd, reliance IIIrd, BSNL IVth, aritel V^{th}, idea VIth, telenor VIIth, tatadocomo VIIIth, and other IXth. Fourth categories ranks as for as namely, Samsung I^{st}, vivo IInd, xiomi IIIrd, oppo IVth, micrimax V^{th}, lenovo VIth, gionee VIIth, HTC VIIIth, LG IXth, lava X^{th}, noki XIth, korbon XIIth, and other XIIIth. Fifth categories ranks as for as namely, jio I^{st}, vodaphone IInd, aritel IIIrd, idea IVth, BSNL V^{th}, reliance VIth, other VIIth. Six categories ranks as for as namely, android mobile I^{st}, and key pad mobile IInd, respectively.

Summary and Conclusions

(XVII) The maximum number of respondents 43.14 % was found having medium level of scientific orientation while 31.48% respondents were found in the categories of high and 25.38% low levels of scientific orientation each, respectively.

2. Knowledge extent of post graduate students about mass media utilization pattern.

(I) The among of mass media utilization pattern uses by the respondents extent of knowledge, and general information sources as well as about various knowledge on mass media utilization pattern. The all information sources were categorized in to seven categories, The majority of first categories ranks at were concerned like mobile/ cell phone/android phone I^{st}, television/L,C.D IInd, agril. books IIIrd, newspapers IVth, laptop/computer V^{th}, radio VIth, exibitions VIIth, pumplets VIIIth, demostration IXth, journals/agril. magazines X^{th}, posters XIth, film shows XIIth, leaflets XIIIth, folders XIVth, and charts XVth. The majority of second categories ranks were concerned like new information collection and spread I^{st}, provide technical knowledge IInd, email IIIrd, proper channel provide for mass communication IVth, internet V^{th}, and to use the social network VIth. The majority of third categories ranks were concerned like entertainment service I^{st}, internet sevice IInd, communication service IIIrd, transfer/ transaction service IVth, give new information related services V^{th}, and help in the research service VIth. The majority of fourth categories ranks were concerned like ATICs (Agriculture Technology Information Centre) I^{st}, Kisan Call Centers provides information to students through direct contact through different mass media pattern provide technical knowledge IInd, Krishi Vigyan Kendras (KVKs) IIIrd, Private agencies IVth, Agriculture department V^{th}, and NGOs VIth. The majority of fifth categories ranks were concerned like Information for better develop new strategies I^{st}, Information about research work IInd, New information for develop the management practices IIIrd, and Information about for change technology knowledge IVth. The majority of six categories ranks were concerned like Whatsapp I^{st}, research work IInd, e-market plus IIIrd, chatting IVth, facebook V^{th}, AGRISNET (Agricultural Informatics and Communication System Network) VIth, AQUA (Almost Questions Answered) VIIth, AGMARKNET (Agricultural Marketing Information System) VIIIth, e-Governace IXth, and e-Choupal X^{th}. The majority of seventh categories ranks were concerned like Help to

Summary and Conclusions

exchange new information anytime the need arose I^{st}, Help to easily send or communicate information anytime the need arose IInd, Increase technology knowledge of students quickly IIIrd, Continuous helps in accumulate current information from accruing area IVth, Assist in obtaining new information quickly V^{th}, and Mostly solve problem quickly VIth, respectively.

(II) The among of mass media utilization pattern users by the respondents extent of knowledge about educational atmosphere in his university, and general information sources as well as about various knowledge on mass media utilization pattern. The all information sources were concerned like. The majority of Library I^{st}, Research work show through projector IInd, teaching through projector IIIrd, ATIC IVth, and Demonstration of field research trial V^{th}, respectively.

(III) The all among respondents extent of knowledge, and general information sources as well as contact in his university various knowledge on mass media utilization pattern. The all information sources were concerned, formal sources rank like. The majority of Advisor I^{st}, Major member IInd, Head of the department IIIrd, Hostel warden IVth, other teacher V^{th}, Dean of college VIth, Registrar VIIth, Vic-chancellor of university VIIIth, Deputy registrar IXth, Placement officer X^{th}, Teacher of other universty XIth, and Any other XIIth, respectively.

3. The utilization pattern of mass media by the students.

(I) The usage of mass media utilization pattern to different purpose by the respondents, general information as well as development the of students about mass media utilization pattern, namely Radio, Television, Laptop/Computer, Newspapers, Agril. Books, Magazines, Mobiles/Cell phone/Android phone, Demonstration, Film show, Exhibition, and Posters. The respondents use different purpose. Radio the majority of respondents (40.60%), was reported having news, followed by entertainment (27.93%), agriculture information (21.32%), and course study (10.15%), television the majority of respondents (48.22%), was reported having news, followed by sport news (27.91%), entertainment (12.69%), discovery/wild life news (6.09%), and movies (5.09%), laptop/computer the majority of respondents (27.91%), was reported having research work,

Summary and Conclusions

followed by entertainment (25.38%), data analysis & collection (17.78%), internet (15.22%), news (8.64%), and playing game (5.07%), newspaper the majority of respondents (38.07%), was reported having national news, followed by state news (22.84%), world news (16.24%), local news (12.69%), and sport news(10.16), agril. books the majority of respondents (48.22%), was reported having preparation, followed by only course examination (22.86%), reading (12.69%), knowledge (11.16%), and agriculture practices managements (5.07%), magazines the majority of respondents (25.38%), was reported having farm management information, followed by animal husbandry development information (22.84%), preparation for the competitive exams (17.76%), farming development (12.69%), entertainment (11.18%), and poultry development information (10.15%), mobile/cell phone/ android phone the majority of respondents (48.22%), was reported having communication, followed by internet (28.95%), entertainment (12.69%), news (5.07%), search abstract & topic (3.04%), and competitive examination (2.03%), demonstratration the majority of respondents (43.14%), was reported having Sowing new practice for student development, followed by Sowing new technical information (22.84%), motivation and stimulate student for action (15.23%), Build confidence about student (11.17%), and improving knowledge (7.62), film shows the majority of respondents (40.61%), was reported having transfer of new technology, followed by transfer of new method for managing farm (27.92%), receive information (21.32%), and entertainment (10.15%), exhibition the majority of respondents (41.62%), was reported having education knowledge development, followed by skill development (24.36%), change behavior (17.76%), attitude development (16.25%), and posters the majority of respondents (43.15%), was reported having display of awareness in classroom, followed by display of technical information in classroom (22.84%), fast receiving message (17.77%), and quick display knowledge gain (16.24%), respectively.

Correlation coefficient (r) between different variables and Knowledge extent about post graduate students.

Table 5.4.1 focuses that the out of 12 variables studied, the variables marital status, family size, material possession, family income, housing pattern, extension contact, and scientific orientation highly significant and positively correlated with knowledge extent about using mass media utilization pattern, the variable like family type, land holding, and social participation, was found significant and positively correlated. The variable like age was found positively correlated with knowledge extent about using mass media utilization pattern and the variable caste only found negatively correlated with knowledge extent about using mass media utilization pattern. Those variables which showed the significant, positive and negative relationship between independents and dependence variables had direct influence overuse of knowledge extent on mass media utilization pattern by the students for his development. It means that if the values variables increase. Knowledge extent about post graduate students will also increase.

Correlation coefficient (r) between different variables and Knowledge extent about mass media utilization pattern to post graduate students.

Out of 12 variables studied, the variable material possession, extension contact and scientific orientation highly significant and possivelity correlated with mass media utilization pattern, the variable like housing pattern and age, marital status, family type, family size, land holding, social participation and family income significant and highly positive correlated. The variable like caste were found negative correlated about mass media utilization pattern using by post graduate students. Those variables which showed the significant, positive and negative relationship between independents and dependence variables had direct influence overuse of knowledge extent about mass media utilization pattern by the post graduate students for his development. It means that if the values variables increase. Knowledge extent about mass media utilization pattern for post graduate students will also increase.

Constraints

Out of the 17 common problem that the maximum number of the respondents 99.49% with adopt a rank of first were agreed with the statements that high cost of internet package for recharging is the common problem, followed by weak slow networking in the university campus 98.98% at rank second, proper not available equipment related to mass media utilization pattern 98.47% at rank third, limited internet

Summary and Conclusions

facilities in universities computer lab 97.46% at rank forth, slow data speed of internet in hostel, department, and college 96.44% at rank fifth, proper literature is not available in the university library 95.93% at rank sixth, lack of light for charging mass media utilization pattern equipments 94.92% at rank seventh, very price full mass media utilization pattern 92.89 % at rank eighth, lack of money for purchase of mass media utilization pattern 90.35% at rank ninth, Wi-Fi facility not available in university campus 88.83% at rank tenth, heavy work load in course study 86.24% at rank eleventh, insufficient technical support 83.75% at rank twelfth, spreading fake news in mobile mass media uses 82.23% at rank thirteenth, lack of time for listen and seen of mass media utilization pattern for gathering information 68.52% at rank fourteenth, lack of proper broadcasting by the mass media utilization pattern 62.43% at rank fifteenth, problem of language when mass media utilization pattern 43.14% at rank sixteenth, and lack of fund within the university building for internet lab 38.07% at rank seventeenth, respectively.

Suggestion

The different suggestive measured as perceived by the respondents. The maximum number of the respondents 99.49 % with adopt a rank of first were agreed with the statements that financial support for purchase of mass media utilization pattern is the common suggestion, followed by proper time given by the students for listen and seen of mass media utilization pattern for gathering information 98.98% at rank second, proper provided light facility for charging mass media utilization pattern equipments 98.47% at rank third, improving networking system in the university campus 97.46% at rank fourth, Wi-Fi facility provided in university campus 96.44% at rank fifth, low cost of internet package for recharging 95.93% at rank sixth, non spreading fake news in mobile mass media uses 92.89% at rank seventh, used simple language when mass media utilization pattern by the students 90.35% at rank eighth, decreasing work load in course study 86.29% at rank ninth, unlimited internet facilities provided by in the universities computer lab 83.75% at rank tenth, sufficient technical support 82.74% at rank eleventh, proper literature is provided by the university library 80.20% at rank twelfth, proper fund provided by the govt. to university building for internet lab 78.68% at rank thirteenth,

Summary and Conclusions

improve networking system in hostel, department, and college 77.64% at rank fourteen, Proper available equipment related to mass media utilization pattern in university campus 76.14% at rank fifteen, mass media utilization pattern available in the market low prices for purchasable about students 75.63% at rank sixteen, and regular broadcasting by the mass media utilization pattern 73.60% at rank seventeen, respectively.

www.ingramcontent.com/pod-product-compliance
Lightning Source LLC
LaVergne TN
LVHW020441070526
838199LV00063B/4804